Practical Approaches to
Literary Criticism

LIBREX—

Longman Group UK Limited,
Longman House, Burnt Mill, Harlow,
Essex CM20 2JE, England
and Associated Companies throughout the world.

© Longman Group UK Limited 1987
First published 1987

Set in 10/12pt Linotron 202 Baskerville
Printed in Hong Kong by

ISBN 0 582 35529 X

This book is for Reggie Alton

Contents

4 Using the theatre: Stage and page 52

5 Playing at life: How plays make us think 86

Chronological table of extracts 102

Acknowledgements 103

Introduction

This book will offer to post-GCSE students a critical framework that will help them to approach the task of discussing play extracts in a confident and informed way.

It is hoped that students will gain a knowledge and appreciation of some of the basic dramatic and structural techniques that are most frequently employed by playwrights, and that this understanding will enable them to describe and analyse their responses to individual passages clearly and logically.

Although a practical approach to drama and theatre arts is beyond the scope of this book, it is still hoped that students will gain from the types of analysis they are encouraged to make here, a fuller appreciation of how an extract might work *within the theatre*.

The focus of the book is on formulating approaches to unseen extracts and on acquiring skills in literary appreciation. Nevertheless, the areas of study that are illustrated here – and the methods of analysis that are suggested – should also be of considerable assistance to students in the study of entire drama texts.

Finally, it is hoped that the range of examples included in this survey will give students a broad sense of dramatic traditions and chronology, and will encourage them to read and/or attend a wider range of plays than they might otherwise have considered.

within the theatre.

texts.

have considered.

1 Opening scenes
In at the deep end

The way in which a play begins is obviously very important. The playwright will need to establish a setting and a mood. Particular characters will have to be introduced. Their situation and relationships to each other must then be indicated. And, in addition, a series of signals will usually be given to the audience or readers to suggest what *sort* of play this is – the kind of action we can expect it to feature, and what its themes and preoccupations are likely to be.

A dramatist has many options in deciding how to open a play. He or she may choose to go 'in at the deep end', beginning in the middle of the action and presenting the reader or audience with a series of puzzles to solve: who are the characters? what are they talking about? what is going on? Alternatively, the dramatist may instead opt to prepare the ground very carefully before the main action, introducing characters slowly and methodically to allow the audience to build up a set of judgements or expectations. *Mood* can also vary. Will the dramatist aim to shock us, to amuse us, or to frighten us, for example?

Bearing these points in mind, read the following passage carefully and then consider the questions printed below it.

A Resounding Tinkle

SCENE   *The living-room of the Paradocks' suburban home. Evening.*

A door back centre leads to a small entrance hall, where coats and hats are hanging. There is a window right of the door, from which anyone standing on the front doorstep can be seen obliquely. A window right looks out on to the garden. The fireplace is left. A

1

sofa stands left centre with a small table left of it, on which there is a radio-receiver. A low coffee-table stands in front of the sofa. On it, there are some rug-making materials. There is an armchair right centre and a sideboard up right. Several bottles are on the sideboard. Small tables stand down right and down left. There is a telephone on the table down left. Built-in bookshelves fill the wall left of the door. A standard lamp is above the window right. In the hall there is a hall-cupboard and a hat-stand with hats and coats on it. Other suitable dressing may be added at the discretion of the Producer.

When the curtain rises, it is not yet dark, and the window curtains are undrawn. A fire is burning in the grate. BRO *and* MIDDIE PARADOCK *have just come in. A shopping basket full of books is on the coffee table. Both* BRO *and* MIDDIE *are staring out of the window right into the garden.*

MIDDIE   It'll have to stay out.

BRO   (*turning away from the window*)   What are the measurements?

MIDDIE   (*continuing to stare through the window*)   You don't need measurements. A thing that size in a semi!

BRO   (*moving to the sideboard*)   I thought we were living in a bungalow. (*He picks up two small adjustable spanners from the sideboard*)

MIDDIE   People think you're trying to go one better than everybody else.

BRO   What are these doing here? When did we order adjustable spanners?   10

MIDDIE   (*without turning*)   They were samples.

BRO   What do think we want with two?

MIDDIE   (*turning away from the window and beginning to put books from the shopping basket on to the bookshelf*)   One of them is probably for loosening things.

BRO   You can do that with any spanner.

MIDDIE   (*with a handful of small identical books*)   I've brought

2

in some more of these in case Uncle Ted comes. I expect he'll ask for critical essays with his coffee.

BRO (*after a pause*) There's no difference between them. 20
You can use either of them for tightening and you can
use either of them for loosening.

(MIDDIE *puts the last book on the shelf, picks up the basket and
moves to the door*)

MIDDIE One is probably bigger than the other or something.

(MIDDIE *exits up centre to left, leaving the door open*)

BRO They're *adjustable*, Middie. (*He puts the spanners on
the sideboard, goes to the armchair right centre, picks up a
newspaper, sits and reads*)

MIDDIE (*off*) Or smaller or something.

BRO The plain fact is that we don't need adjustable
spanners and are never likely to. (*He pauses*) It would
be interesting to know what would have happened if
I'd answered the door and let them foist adjustable 30
spanners on to us.

MIDDIE (*off*) We don't have to use them if we don't like
them.

BRO (*after a pause*) We shall have them unloading a com-
plete tool-kit on us before we know where we are.

MIDDIE (*off*) They won't be round again.

BRO I hope you're right – that's all I can say.

MIDDIE (*off*) I wish it were.

(MIDDIE *enters up centre from left, and as though attracted com-
pulsively towards it, crosses to the window right*)

I wish that were all you could say. Except that then
we'd have you saying it all day long. I suppose, like a 40
mentally deficient parakeet. (*She looks steadily through the
window*)

BRO What a typical woman's remark. A parakeet saying

the same thing over and over again wouldn't necessarily be mentally deficient. If that's all it's been taught
how can it say anything different?

MIDDIE Look at it.

BRO It may be educationally subnormal – but that's
another matter.

MIDDIE Look at its great ears flapping about.

BRO (*after a pause*) It's only once a year for goodness'   50
sake.

MIDDIE Surely they know by now what size we always
have.

BRO Perhaps they've sent us the wrong one.

MIDDIE (*crossing above the armchair to the sofa*) It's big
enough for a hotel. (*She picks up a magazine from the
coffee-table and sits on the sofa*) If you had a hotel or a
private school or something you wouldn't need a thing
that size. (*She looks through the magazine*)

BRO I suppose not.   60

MIDDIE And supposing it goes berserk in the night? I'm
not getting up to it.

BRO Why should it go berserk any more than a smaller
one?

MIDDIE We shall have old Mrs Stencil round again if it
does – threatening us with the R.S.P.C.A.

BRO You should have been in when they came with it,
then you could have queried the measurements.

MIDDIE I can't think what we're going to call it. We
can't call it Mr. Trench again.   70

BRO The only time we've not called it Mr. Trench was
three years ago when we had to make do with a giraffe.

MIDDIE And look at the fuss we had before they'd take it
in part exchange.

BRO Of course they made a fuss. There was something
wrong with it.

N F Simpson (Faber & Faber, 1957)

1   What impression do you form of the Paradocks from the house in which they live?
2   What is the 'it' in line 1?
3   What does the conversation about adjustable spanners suggest to you about the couple? What is the effect of such a conversation at this stage in the action?
4   What details about the Paradocks' life and behaviour strike you as extraordinary?
5   Can you suggest why this couple are called the 'Paradocks'?
6   What overall effect does this opening passage have on you? What kind of play does it lead you to expect? What do you imagine will happen next?

The previous extract might well be described as an example of an opening scene that goes 'in at the deep end', in that it plunges us straight into an unfamiliar situation without preparation or explanation. As an example of a first scene that provides a significantly greater degree of background information (although in a very complex and subtle way), look carefully at the opening of Shakespeare's *Antony and Cleopatra* below. The scene is set in Alexandria, the Egyptian capital, and Cleopatra is Egypt's queen. To be with her, Antony, a famous Roman general and one of the three rulers of ancient Rome, has deserted his wife, Fulvia. The scene opens and closes with comments about the situation by Demetrius and Philo, two Roman soldiers, who are friends of Antony.

Antony and Cleopatra

Enter DEMETRIUS *and* PHILO

PHILO
    Nay, but this dotage of our general's
    O'erflows the measure: those his goodly eyes,

That o'er the files and musters of the war
Have glow'd like plated Mars, now bend, now turn
The office and devotion of their view
Upon a tawny front: his captain's heart,
Which in the scuffles of great fights hath burst
The buckles on his breast, reneges all temper,
And is become the bellows and the fan
To cool a gipsy's lust.

Flourish. Enter ANTONY, CLEOPATRA, *her Ladies, the Train,
with Eunuchs fanning her.*

                    Look, where they come: 10
Take but good note, and you shall see in him
The triple pillar of the world transform'd
Into a strumpet's fool: behold and see.

CLEOPATRA

If it be love indeed, tell me how much.

ANTONY

There's beggary in the love that can be reckon'd.

CLEOPATRA

I'll set a bourn how far to be belov'd.

ANTONY

Then must thou needs find out new heaven, new earth.

ATTENDANT

News, my good lord, from Rome.

ANTONY

                        Grates me, the sum.

CLEOPATRA

Nay, hear them, Antony:
Fulvia perchance is angry; or who knows   20
If the scarce-bearded Caesar have not sent
His powerful mandate to you, 'Do this, or this;

Take in that kingdom, and enfranchise that;
Perform't, or else we damn thee.'

ANTONY

How, my love?

CLEOPATRA

Perchance? nay, and most like:
You must not stay here longer, your dismission
Is come from Caesar, therefore hear it, Antony.
Where's Fulvia's process? Caesar's I would say. Both?
Call in the messengers. As I am Egypt's queen,
Thou blushest, Antony, and that blood of thine   30
Is Caesar's homager: else so thy cheek pays shame
When shrill-tongued Fulvia scolds. The messengers!

ANTONY

Let Rome in Tiber melt, and the wide arch
Of the rang'd empire fall! Here is my space,
Kingdoms are clay: our dungy earth alike
Feeds beast as man; the nobleness of life
Is to do thus: when such a mutual pair, (*embracing*)
And such a twain can do't, in which I bind,
On pain of punishment, the world to weet
We stand up peerless.

CLEOPATRA

Excellent falsehood!   40
Why did he marry Fulvia, and not love her?
I'll seem the fool I am not; Antony
Will be himself.

ANTONY

But stirr'd by Cleopatra.
Now for the love of Love, and her soft hours,
Let's not confound the time with conference harsh:
There's not a minute of our lives should stretch
Without some pleasure now. What sport to-night?

CLEOPATRA

Hear the ambassadors.

ANTONY

        Fie, wrangling queen!
Whom every thing becomes, to chide, to laugh,
To weep: how every passion fully strives   50
To make itself, in thee, fair and admired!
No messenger but thine, and all alone,
To-night we'll wander through the streets, and note
The qualities of people. Come, my queen,
Last night you did desire it. Speak not to us.

   Exeunt ANTONY *and* CLEOPATRA *with their Train*

DEMETRIUS

Is Caesar with Antonius priz'd so slight?

PHILO

Sir, sometimes, when he is not Antony,
He comes too short of that great property
Which still should go with Antony.

DEMETRIUS

       I am full sorry
That he approves the common liar, who   60
Thus speaks of him at Rome; but I will hope
Of better deeds to-morrow. Rest you happy!

          Exeunt
   William Shakespeare (1607)

Now consider the following questions. Those at the end
marked with asterisks are for students familiar with the whole
play.

1 Why does Philo disapprove of Antony's behaviour?
2 What image of Antony and Cleopatra does he create for us
 in his opening speech?

8

3 What impression do you yourself form from this scene of Antony and Cleopatra and their relationship? How likeable do you find them?
4 How do the characters' different ways of speaking bring out the differences between Roman and Egyptian viewpoints?
5 Would this opening scene have worked as well *without* Philo's first speech? Give your reasons.
6 What ending do you imagine for the play, on the basis of this opening?
7* Give examples of other scenes in the play in which the different lifestyles of Rome and Egypt are contrasted.
8* Do you consider Antony's and Cleopatra's behaviour here to be consistent with their behaviour in the rest of the play?

The final two extracts in this section are included to show the different *moods* that a playwright may choose to establish.

Riders to the Sea

Cottage kitchen, with nets, oilskins, spinning-wheel, some new boards standing by the wall, etc. Cathleen, a girl of about twenty, finishes kneading cake, and puts it down in the pot-oven by the fire; then wipes her hands, and begins to spin at the wheel. Nora, a young girl, puts her head in at the door.

NORA (*In a low voice*) Where is she?
CATHLEEN She's lying down, God help her, and maybe sleeping, if she's able.

Nora comes in softly, and takes a bundle from under her shawl.

CATHLEEN (*Spinning the wheel rapidly*) What is it you have?
NORA The young priest is after bringing them. It's a shirt and a plain stocking were got off a drowned man in Donegal.

9

Cathleen stops her wheel with a sudden movement, and leans out to listen.

NORA We're to find out if it's Michael's they are, some time herself will be down looking by the sea.

CATHLEEN How would they be Michael's, Nora? How   10
would he go the length of that way to the far north?

NORA The young priest says he's known the like of it. 'If it's Michael's they are,' says he, 'you can tell herself he's got a clean burial, by the grace of God; and if they're not his, let no one say a word about them, for she'll be getting her death,' says he, 'with crying and lamenting.'

The door which Nora half closed is blown open by a gust of wind.

CATHLEEN (*looking out anxiously*) Did you ask him would he stop Bartley going this day with the horses to the Galway fair?
                                                                    20

NORA 'I won't stop him,' says he; 'but let you not be afraid. Herself does be saying prayers half through the night, and the Almighty God won't leave her destitute,' says he, 'with no son living.'

CATHLEEN Is the sea bad by the white rocks, Nora?

NORA Middling bad, God help us. There's a great roaring in the west, and it's worse it'll be getting when the tide's turned to the wind. (*She goes over to the table with the bundle*) Shall I open it now?

CATHLEEN Maybe she'd wake up on us, and come in   30
before we'd done. (*Coming to the table*) It's a long time we'll be, and the two of us crying.

NORA (*goes to the inner door and listens*) She's moving about on the bed. She'll be coming in a minute.

CATHLEEN Give me the ladder, and I'll put them up in the turf loft, the way she won't know of them at all, and maybe when the tide turns she'll be going down to see would he be floating from the east.

*They put the ladder against the gable of the chimney; Cathleen
goes up a few steps and hides the bundle in the turf loft. Maurya
comes from the inner room.*

John Millington Synge (1905)

1 What do we learn about the old woman, Maurya, before
   her entrance? What has happened to her son, Michael?
   What is her son Bartley about to do?
2 Why does Cathleen hide the bundle of clothes?
3 What mood is evoked by this opening? What do you expect
   to happen later in the play?
4 How does Synge make his audience strongly aware of the
   presence of the sea in this extract. What impression do you
   form of the sea?
5 How helpful are the comments of the young priest?
6 To what extent does the Irish dialect spoken by the characters contribute to the play's atmosphere?

The Philanthropist

PHILIP'S *room. The room of a bachelor don, comfortable but not
well-furnished, ordered but not tidy.* PHILIP *and* DONALD *sit relaxed but attentive, one in an armchair, one on the sofa perhaps.*
JOHN, *a younger man, is sitting in a wooden chair, a pile of
papers on his knee. He holds a revolver.*

JOHN   You needn't think I'm not serious. Because I am.
   I assure you I am. Can't you see that? I've come here
   this evening because I think both of you are responsible for this and I think you deserve it as much as I
   do. If you hate me for doing it, that's your problem. It
   won't concern me. I just want you to have one vivid
   image of me, that's all, one memory to last all your life
   and never vanish, to remind you that if you won, I lost,

and that nobody can win without somebody losing. Good-bye. (*He puts the revolver to his head.*) Bang. (*He smiles uneasily at them.*) Curtain. 10
(*Silence.*)
Do you like it?

PHILIP Very good. Would you like another drink?

JOHN Oh, yes, thanks, er . . . Philip.

PHILIP *pours a drink*.

PHILIP Ice?

JOHN Please.

Exit PHILIP

JOHN He doesn't like it, does he?

DON Oh, I don't know.

JOHN He doesn't. I can tell.

DON I'm sure he does like it. 20

PHILIP *returns with the ice.*

DON Well. Yes and no. I mean there are some enor-
mously promising things in the play. Obviously it's
basically a conversation piece, but you do try to give
the customers a bit of everything – a touch of melo-
drama, the odd *coup de théâtre*, humour, tragedy, mono-
logues and pastoral interludes, yes, yes, I like that,
generous. But on the other hand I think there are certain . . . lapses, which, you know, detract from the play
as a satisfying whole.

JOHN You mean it's stylistically heterogeneous? 30

PHILIP I think Don prefers to see it as an unsatisfying
whole. (*He laughs merrily and alone.*) Sorry. Would you
like a chocolate?

JOHN No, thanks.

PHILIP Don? I think I'll have one.

He helps himself to one, as he is to throughout this scene.

JOHN Tell me what you don't like about it.

DON Well, one thing is that character who appears every so often with a ladder. The window-cleaner. What's his name?

JOHN Man.   40

DON Yes. Well, I take it he has some kind of allegorical significance outside the framework of the play. I mean I don't know if this is right but I rather look him to signify England.

JOHN No, no, erm, in point of fact he signifies man.

DON Ah.

JOHN Yes.

DON Hence the name.

JOHN Yes.

DON I see.   50

JOHN Although now you come to mention it, I suppose he could be taken to represent England.

Christopher Hampton (Faber & Faber, 1970)

1 What is the effect on an audience of John's opening speech?
2 How would you describe the mood of this opening?
3 What is your attitude to the three characters and their world?
4 What sort of a play would you expect to follow such an opening?

Assignment

Compare the opening scene of Shakespeare's *Antony and Cleopatra* (see pages 5–8) with the opening scene *All For Love* (1678) by John Dryden.

2 Presenting characters How people reveal themselves

A playwright may use many different methods of characterisation in order to establish what he or she sees as the important facts about the people around whom the play's drama revolves. At one extreme, indeed, the dramatist may even issue very explicit stage directions that define precisely how he or she intends the characters to be interpreted and represented on stage. An example of this kind of authorial direction can be seen in the stage directions to *Look Back in Anger* by John Osborne, where the three main characters are described in the following way.

Look Back in Anger

At rise of curtain, JIMMY *and* CLIFF *are seated in the two armchairs, right and left, respectively. All that we can see of either of them is two pairs of legs, sprawled way out beyond the newspapers which hide the rest of them from sight. They are both reading. Beside them, and between them, is a jungle of newspapers and weeklies. When we do eventually see them, we find that* JIMMY *is a tall, thin young man about twenty-five, wearing a very worn tweed jacket and flannels. Clouds of smoke fill the room from the pipe he is smoking. He is a disconcerting mixture of sincerity and cheerful malice, of tenderness and freebooting cruelty; restless, importunate, full of pride, a combination which alienates the sensitive and insensitive alike. Blistering honesty, or apparent honesty, like his, makes few friends. To many he may seem insensitive to the point of vulgarity. To others, he is simply a loudmouth. To be as vehement as he is is to be almost non-committal.*

10

CLIFF *is the same age, short, dark, big boned, wearing a pullover and grey, new, but very creased trousers. He is easy and relaxed, almost to lethargy, with the rather sad, natural intelligence of the self-taught. If* JIMMY *alienates love,* CLIFF *seems to exact it – demonstrations of it, at least, even from the cautious. He is a* 20 *soothing, natural counterpoint to* JIMMY.

Standing left, below the food cupboard, is ALISON. *She is leaning over an ironing board. Beside her is a pile of clothes. Hers is the most elusive personality to catch in the uneasy polyphony of these three people. She is turned in a different key, a key of well-bred malaise that is often drowned in the robust orchestration of the other two. Hanging over the grubby, but expensive, skirt she is wearing is a cherry red shirt of* JIMMY'S, *but she manages some-how to look quite elegant in it. She is roughly the same age as the men. Somehow, their combined physical oddity makes her beauty* 30 *more striking than it really is. She is tall, slim, dark. The bones of her face are long and delicate. There is a surprising reservation about her eyes, which are so large and deep they should make equivocation impossible.*

John Osborne (Faber & Faber, 1956)

1   Which comments here represent the *author's* view of the characters?
2   Which comments suggest how the characters might appear to others?
3   What comparisons between characters does Osborne make here?

In general, however, so immediately prescriptive an approach to character definition is comparatively rare among dramatists. Most prefer the other methods of characterisation (which Osborne also uses) which encourage the director, reader, actor or viewer to interpret the characters' personalities and motives for him- or herself. These methods include defining a character by how he or she *looks*, by how he or she *speaks*, by what other people say *about* that character, and by what the character *says* and *does*.

Appearance

The clothes that Jimmy, Cliff and Alison wear in the above extract are deliberately specified by Osborne in order to suggest certain things about their personalities and relationships with one another. Below are three playwrights' comments on characters' dress. What sort of a person does each of the following stage directions lead you to expect?

Arms and the Man

Catherine Petkoff, a woman over forty, imperiously energetic, with magnificent black hair and eyes, who might be a very splendid specimen of the wife of a mountain farmer, but is determined to be a Viennese lady, and to that end wears a fashionable tea gown on all occasions.

George Bernard Shaw (1898)

The Last of My Solid Gold Watches

The door opens and MR CHARLIE COLTON *comes in. He is a legendary character, seventy-eight years old but still 'going strong'. He is lavish of flesh, superbly massive and with a kingly dignity of bearing. Once he moved with a tidal ease and power. Now he puffs and rumbles; when no one is looking he clasps his hand to his chest and cocks his head to the warning heart inside him. His huge expanse of chest and belly is criss-crossed by multiple gold chains with various little fobs and trinkets suspended from them. On the back of his head is a derby and in his mouth a cigar.*

Tennessee Williams (E Green (Publishers) Ltd, 1948)

Krapp's Last Tape

Sitting at the table, facing front, i.e. across from the drawers, a wearish old man: KRAPP.

Rusty black narrow trousers too short for him. Rusty black sleeveless waistcoat, four capacious pockets. Heavy silver watch and chain. Grimy white shirt open at neck, no collar. Surprising pair of dirty white boots, size ten at least, very narrow and pointed.

White face. Purple nose. Disordered grey hair. Unshaven.

Very near sighted (but unspectacled). Hard of hearing.

Cracked voice. Distinctive intonation.

Samuel Beckett (Faber & Faber, 1958)

How characters speak

Clearly, the type of vocabulary and verbal structures that a character uses to express him- or herself will give us many indications about that person's age, background, attitudes and personality. What assumptions are you prompted to make about the following characters, for example, simply on the basis of how they speak?

Jumpers

To begin at the beginning: is God? (*Pause.*) I prefer to put the question in this form because to ask, 'Does God exist?' appears to presuppose the existence of a God who may not, and I do not propose this late evening to follow my friend Russell, this evening to follow my late friend Russell, to follow my good friend the late Lord Russell, necrophiliac rubbish!, to begin at the beginning: is God? (*He ponders a moment.*) To ask, 'Is God?' appears to presuppose a Being who perhaps isn't . . . and thus is open

17

to the same objection as the question, 'Does God exist?'   10
. . . but until the difficulty is pointed out it does not have
the same propensity to confuse language with meaning
and to conjure up a God who may have any number of
predicates including omniscience, perfection and four-
wheel-drive but not, as it happens, existence. This
confusion, which indicates only that language is an
approximation of meaning and not a logical symbolism
for it, began with Plato and was not ended by Bertrand
Russell's theory that existence could only be asserted of
descriptions and not of individuals, but I do not propose   20
this evening to follow into the Theory of Descriptions my
very old friend – now dead, of course – *ach!* – to follow
into the Theory of Descriptions, the late Lord Russell—!

Tom Stoppard (Faber & Faber, 1972)

Roots

Oh, *he* thinks we count all right – living in mystic communion with nature. Living in mystic bloody communion
with nature (indeed). But us count? Count Mother? I
wonder. Do we? Do you think we really count? You don'
wanna take any notice of what them ole papers say about
the workers bein' all-important these days – that's all
squit! 'Cos we aren't. Do you think when the really
talented people in the country get to work they get to
work for us? Hell if they do! Do you think they don't
know we 'ont make the effort? The writers don't write   10
thinkin' we can understand, nor the painters don't paint
expecting us to be interested – that they don't, nor don't
the composers give out music thinking we can appreciate
it. 'Blust,' they say, 'the masses is too stupid for us to
come down to them. Blust,' they say, 'if they don't make
no effort why should we bother?' So you know who come
along? The slop singers and the pop writers and the film

makers and women's magazines and the Sunday papers
and the picture strip love stories – that's who come along,
and you don't have to make no effort for them, it come   20
easy. 'We know where the money lie,' they say, 'hell we
do! The workers've got it so let's give them what they
want. If they want slop songs and film idols we'll give
'em that then. If they want the third-rate, *blust!* We'll
give 'em *that* then. Anything's good enough for them 'cos
they don't ask for no more!' The whole stinkin' commer-
cial world insults us and we don't care a damn. Well,
Ronnie's right – it's our own bloody fault. We want the
third-rate – we got it! We got it! We got it! We . . .

Arnold Wesker (Penguin, 1959)

As a more sustained example of how language can express
character, look carefully at the following extract from
Shakespeare's *A Midsummer Night's Dream*. The scene is set in
an enchanted wood near Athens. Bottom is an Athenian work-
man who, with his friends, has been practising in the wood for
an amateur play production. Puck, a mischievous spirit, has
cast a spell placing an ass's head on Bottom. The other work-
men flee in panic, but Bottom is unaware that anything is
wrong and thinks they are playing a joke on him. Meanwhile,
Titania (the Queen of the fairies) has been placed under a spell
which means that she will fall in love with the first creature she
sees on awakening.

A Midsummer Night's Dream

BOTTOM
Why do they run away? this is a knavery of them to
make me afeard.

Re-enter SNOUT

SNOUT

O Bottom, thou art changed! what do I see on thee?

BOTTOM

What do you see? you see an ass-head of your own, do you?

Exit SNOUT

Re-enter QUINCE

QUINCE

Bless thee, Bottom! bless thee! thou art translated.

Exit

BOTTOM

I see their knavery: this is to make an ass of me; to fright me, if they could. But I will not stir from this place, do what they can: I will walk up and down here, and I will sing, that they shall hear I am not afraid. 10 (*Sings*)

> The ousel-cock so black of hue,
>> With orange-tawny bill,
> The throstle with his note so true,
>> The wren with little quill, –

TITANIA (*Awaking*)

What angel wakes me from my flowery bed?

BOTTOM (*Sings*)

> The finch, the sparrow, and the lark,
>> The plain-song cuckoo gray,
> Whose note full many a man doth mark,
>> And dares not answer nay; –

for, indeed, who would set his wit to so foolish a bird? 20 who would give a bird the lie, though he cry 'cuckoo' never so?

TITANIA

I pray thee, gentle mortal, sing again:
Mine ear is much enamour'd of thy note;

So is mine eye enthralled to thy shape;
And thy fair virtue's force perforce doth move me,
On the first view, to say, to swear, I love thee.

BOTTOM

Methinks, mistress, you should have little reason for
that: and yet, to say the truth, reason and love keep
little company together now-a-days; the more the pity   30
that some honest neighbours will not make them
friends. Nay, I can gleek upon occasion.

TITANIA

Thou art as wise as thou art beautiful.

BOTTOM

Not so, neither: but if I had wit enough to get out of
this wood, I have enough to serve mine own turn.

TITANIA

Out of this wood do not desire to go:
Thou shalt remain here, whether thou wilt or no.
I am a spirit of no common rate:
The summer still doth tend upon my state;
And I do love thee: therefore, go with me;   40
I'll give thee fairies to attend on thee;
And they shall fetch thee jewels from the deep,
And sing, while thou on pressed flowers dost sleep:
And I will purge thy mortal grossness so,
That thou shalt like an airy spirit go.
Pease-blossom! Cobweb! Moth! and Mustard-seed!

William Shakespeare (1596)

1 Explain what makes this encounter so amusing.
2 What contrast is established by the fact that Bottom speaks
   primarily in prose, whereas Titania speaks in verse?
3 How is Bottom's song different from the type of poetry
   spoken by Titania?

4 What differences are there in the types of language spoken by these two characters?

5 Which character do you think shows the most dignity in this exchange?

6* To what extent is the behaviour of Bottom and Titania here typical of their behaviour in the rest of *A Midsummer Night's Dream*?

7* Using this extract and referring also to other episodes in the play, show how Shakespeare uses the language of the 'fairy' characters to convey the atmosphere of the enchanted wood.

How characters are described by others

Inevitably, our response to a character is conditioned to some extent by what we may have heard about that person before he or she actually appears. Below, for example, is an extract from *The Browning Version* by Terence Rattigan. The play is set in a very traditional English public school. Frank Hunter (a young schoolmaster) and John Taplow (a pupil) are discussing one of the senior masters, Andrew Crocker-Harris, whom the audience has not yet seen.

The Browning Version

FRANK   I must admit I envy him the effect he seems to have on you boys in his form. You all seem scared to death of him. What does he do – beat you all, or something?

TAPLOW   (*rising and moving to the left end of the settee*)   Good Lord, no. He's not a sadist, like one or two of the others.

FRANK   I beg your pardon?

TAPLOW   A sadist, sir, is someone who gets pleasure out
of giving pain.   10
FRANK   Indeed? But I think you went on to say that
some other masters . . .
TAPLOW   Well, of course they are, sir. I won't mention
names, but you know them as well as I do. Of course I
know most masters think we boys don't understand a
thing – but dash it, sir, you're different. You're young
– well comparatively anyway – and you're science and
you canvassed for Labour in the last election. You
must know what sadism is.

FRANK *stares for a moment at* TAPLOW, *then turns away.*

FRANK   Good Lord! What are public schools coming to?   20
TAPLOW (*crossing to right of the desk, below the chair, and leaning against it*)   Anyway, the Crock isn't a sadist. That's
what I'm saying. He wouldn't be so frightening if he
were – because at least it would show he had some
feelings. But he hasn't. He's all shrivelled up inside like
a nut and he seems to hate people to like him. It's
funny, that. I don't know any other master who
doesn't like being liked.
FRANK   And I don't know any boy who doesn't trade on
that very foible.
TAPLOW   Well, it's natural, sir. But not with the Crock.   30
FRANK (*making a feeble attempt at re-establishing the correct relationship*)   Mr. Crocker-Harris.
TAPLOW   Mr. Crocker-Harris. The funny thing is that in
spite of everything, I do rather like him. I can't help it.
And sometimes I think he sees it and that seems to
shrivel him up even more.
FRANK   I'm sure you're exaggerating.
TAPLOW   No, sir. I'm not. In form the other day he
made one of his little classical jokes. Of course nobody
laughed because nobody understood it, myself included. Still, I knew he'd meant it as funny, so I   40

23

laughed. Not out of sucking-up, sir, I swear, but ordinary common politeness, and feeling a bit sorry for him having made a dud joke. (*He moves round below the desk to left of it.*) Now I can't remember what the joke was – but let's say it was – (*mimicking*) Benedictus, benedicatur, benedictine . . . Now, you laugh, sir.

FRANK *laughs formally.* TAPLOW *looks at him over an imaginary pair of spectacles, and then, very gently crooks his fore-finger to him in indication to approach the table.* FRANK *rises. He is genuinely interested in the incident.*

(*In a gentle, throaty voice.*) Taplow – you laughed at my little pun, I noticed. I must confess I am flattered at the evident advance your Latinity has made that you should so readily have understood what the rest of the form did not. Perhaps, now, you would be good enough to explain it to them, so that they too can share your pleasure.

Terence Rattigan
(Hamish Hamilton/Samuel French, 1948)

1 What do you learn from this extract about Mr Crocker-Harris and his pupils' attitude towards him?
2 Why do you suppose he is nicknamed 'the Crock'?
3 What extra detail about Mr Crocker-Harris is provided by Taplow's mimicking?
4 Do you expect to like him as a character?

The above passage concentrated on *one* person's perception of another character. In the following extract, however, *two* differing perspectives on a character are supplied. The character then enters, and the audience is given the opportunity to form its own judgement. The extract is taken from near the very beginning of *She Stoops to Conquer* by Oliver Goldsmith, and is set in the country house of Mr and Mrs Hardcastle. Read the passage carefully, and then consider the questions that follow it.

She Stoops to Conquer

MRS HARDCASTLE Ay, your times were fine times indeed; you have been telling us of them for many a long year. Here we live in an old rumbling mansion, that looks for all the world like an inn, but that we never see company. Our best visitors are old Mrs Oddfish, the curate's wife, and little Cripplegate, the lame dancing-master; and all our entertainment, your old stories of Prince Eugene and the Duke of Marlborough. I hate such old-fashioned trumpery.

HARDCASTLE And I love it. I love everything that's old: 10 old friends, old times, old manners, old books, old wine; and I believe, Dorothy (*taking her hand*), you'll own I have been pretty fond of an old wife.

MRS HARDCASTLE Lord, Mr Hardcastle, you're for ever at your Dorothy's, and your old wife's! You may be a Darby, but I'll be no Joan, I promise you. I'm not so old as you would make me by more than one good year. Add twenty to twenty, and make money of that.

HARDCASTLE Let me see; twenty added to twenty makes just fifty and seven. 20

MRS HARDCASTLE It's false, Mr Hardcastle: I was but twenty when I was brought to bed of Tony, that I had by Mr Lumpkin, my first husband; and he's not come to years of discretion yet.

HARDCASTLE Nor ever will, I dare answer for him. Ay, you have taught *him* finely.

MRS HARDCASTLE No matter; Tony Lumpkin has a good fortune. My son is not to live by his learning. I don't think a boy wants much learning to spend fifteen hundred a year. 30

HARDCASTLE Learning, quotha! A mere composition of tricks and mischief.

MRS HARDCASTLE Humour, my dear: nothing but humour. Come, Mr Hardcastle, you must allow the boy a little humour.

HARDCASTLE I'd sooner allow him a horse-pond. If burning the footmen's shoes, frighting the maids, and worrying the kittens, be humour, he has it. It was but yesterday he fastened my wig to the back of my chair, and when I went to make a bow, I popped my bald head in Mrs Frizzle's face.   40

MRS HARDCASTLE And am I to blame? The poor boy was always too sickly to do any good. A school would be his death. When he comes to be a little stronger, who knows what a year or two's Latin may do for him?

HARDCASTLE Latin for him! A cat and fiddle! No, no, the alehouse and the stable are the only schools he'll ever go to.

MRS HARDCASTLE Well, we must not snub the poor boy now, for I believe we shan't have him long among us.   50 Anybody that looks in his face may see he's consumptive.

HARDCASTLE Ay, if growing too fat be one of the symptoms.

MRS HARDCASTLE He coughs sometimes.

HARDCASTLE Yes, when his liquor goes the wrong way.

MRS HARDCASTLE I'm actually afraid of his lungs.

HARDCASTLE And truly so am I; for he sometimes whoops like a speaking-trumpet.

(TONY *halloos off stage right*)

O there he goes – a very consumptive figure truly.   60

(TONY LUMPKIN *enters right, crossing the stage*)

MRS HARDCASTLE Tony, where are you going, my charmer? Won't you give papa and I a little of your company, lovee?

TONY I'm in haste, mother, I can't stay.

MRS HARDCASTLE You shan't venture out this raw evening, my dear; you look most shockingly.

TONY I can't stay, I tell you. *The Three Pigeons* expects

me down every moment. There's some fun going forward.

HARDCASTLE   Ay; the alehouse, the old place: I thought   70
so.

MRS HARDCASTLE   A low, paltry set of fellows.

TONY   Not so low, neither. There's Dick Muggins the Exciseman, Jack Slang the horse doctor, little Aminadab that grinds the music box, and Tom Twist that spins the pewter platter.

MRS HARDCASTLE   Pray, my dear, disappoint them for one night at least.

TONY   As for disappointing *them*, I should not so much mind; but I can't abide to disappoint *myself*.   80

MRS HARDCASTLE (*detaining him*)   You shan't go.

TONY   I will, I tell you.

MRS HARDCASTLE   I say you shan't.

TONY   We'll see which is strongest, you or I.

Oliver Goldsmith (1773)

1 What impression do you gain from this extract of the characters of Mr and Mrs Hardcastle?

2 What is Mrs Hardcastle's attitude towards her son?

3 In what ways is this view of him contradicted by Mr Hardcastle?

4 Based on Tony Lumpkin's behaviour when he appears, which assessment do you consider to be the more accurate?

5 What do you learn from this passage about the relationship between mother and son?

What characters say and do

What is revealed by characters' own words and actions is the final aspect of characterisation that will be considered in this section. As an example, read carefully the following passage from *The Duchess of Malfi* by John Webster. The Duchess – whose only 'crime' was to re-marry after the death of her first husband – has been imprisoned by her wicked brothers and believes her second husband to be dead. Cariola is her faithful lady-in-waiting; Bosola is a treacherous servant, in the pay of her brothers.

The Duchess of Malfi

DUCHESS

                      Farewell Cariola,
In my last will I have not much to give;
A many hungry guests have fed upon me,
Thine will be a poor reversion.

CARIOLA

                          I will die with her.

DUCHESS

I pray thee look thou giv'st my little boy
Some syrup for his cold, and let the girl
Say her prayers, ere she sleep.

                       CARIOLA *is forced off*
                    Now what you please,
What death?

BOSOLA

Strangling: here are your executioners.

DUCHESS

I forgive them:
The apoplexy, catarrh, or cough o'th' lungs   10
Would do as much as they do.

BOSOLA

Doth not death fright you?

DUCHESS

      Who would be afraid on't?
Knowing to meet such excellent company
In th'other world.

BOSOLA

     Yet, methinks,
The manner of your death should much afflict you,
This cord should terrify you?

DUCHESS

      Not a whit:
What would it pleasure me, to have my throat cut
With diamonds? or to be smothered
With cassia? or to be shot to death, with pearls?
I know death hath ten thousand several doors 20
For men to take their *Exits*: and 'tis found
They go on such strange geometrical hinges,
You may open them both ways: any way, for Heaven
  sake,
So I were out of your whispering. Tell my brothers
That I perceive death, now I am well awake,
Best gift is, they can give, or I can take.
I would fain put off my last woman's fault,
I'll'd not be tedious to you.

EXECUTIONERS

     We are ready.

DUCHESS

Dispose my breath how please you, but my body
Bestow upon my women, will you?

EXECUTIONERS

      Yes. 30

DUCHESS

Pull, and pull strongly, for your able strength
Must pull down heaven upon me:

29

Yet stay, heaven gates are not so highly arch'd
As princes' palaces: they that enter there
Must go upon their knees. Come violent death,
Serve for mandragora to make me sleep;
Go tell my brothers, when I am laid out,
They then may feed in quiet.

They strangle her

BOSOLA

Where's the waiting woman?
Fetch her. Some other strangle the children.

John Webster (1614)

1 What do you learn about the Duchess's character by her words and behaviour to the other characters in this extract?
2 What further aspects of her nature are shown by her references to her children and to her brothers?
3 What is revealed here by the Duchess's attitude towards death?
4 Show how the Duchess's natural grace and dignity are reflected in the poetry of her speeches in this extract.
5* How does the Duchess's behaviour in this extract compare with her behaviour earlier in the play?
6* Do you find Bosola's attitude in this extract in any way surprising?

Few readers or audiences would doubt the sincerity of the Duchess of Malfi's words in the above extract. Yet it is worth remembering, nevertheless, that what a character says cannot necessarily *always* be taken at face value.

We may reasonably expect words spoken by a character in soliloquy (that is, alone or unheard by others) to represent that character's true feelings. In Shakespeare's great tragedies, for instance, the audience frequently enters the private thoughts of both the heroes (such as Macbeth) and the villains (such as

Iago in *Othello* or Edmund in *King Lear*). But words spoken by a character to or for a specific audience could well be designed to deceive or manipulate, and this is something that should be borne in mind. The extract below is a famous example of the way in which apparent frankness can in fact be extremely carefully calculated.

This passage comes from Shakespeare's *Julius Caesar*. Julius Caesar, the ruler of Rome, has been assassinated by a group of conspirators (led by Brutus and Cassius) who saw him as a dangerous tyrant. Mark Antony, his friend, has been given permission by Brutus to address the crowd at Caesar's funeral on condition that he does not criticise the conspirators. Read the speech carefully, and then answer the questions that follow it.

Julius Caesar

ANTONY

> Friends, Romans, countrymen, lend me your ears;
> I come to bury Caesar, not to praise him.
> The evil that men do lives after them,
> The good is oft interrèd with their bones;
> So let it be with Caesar. The noble Brutus
> Hath told you Caesar was ambitious;
> If it were so, it was a grievous fault,
> And grievously hath Caesar answered it.
> Here, under leave of Brutus and the rest –
> For Brutus is an honourable man,   10
> So are they all, all honourable men –
> Come I to speak in Caesar's funeral.
> He was my friend, faithful and just to me;
> But Brutus says he was ambitious,
> And Brutus is an honourable man.
> He hath brought many captives home to Rome,
> Whose ransoms did the general coffers fill:

Did this in Caesar seem ambitious?
When that the poor have cried, Caesar hath wept;
Ambition should be made of sterner stuff;   20
Yet Brutus says he was ambitious,
And Brutus is an honourable man.
You all did see that on the Lupercal
I thrice presented him a kingly crown,
Which he did thrice refuse. Was this ambition?
Yet Brutus says he was ambitious,
And sure he is an honourable man.
I speak not to disprove what Brutus spoke,
But here I am to speak what I do know.
You all did love him once, not without cause;   30
What cause withholds you then to mourn for him?
O judgement, thou art fled to brutish beasts,
And men have lost their reason. Bear with me;
My heart is in the coffin there with Caesar,
And I must pause till it come back to me.

William Shakespeare (1599)

1   What is the effect of the words 'Friends' (line 1) and 'If it
    were so' (line 7)?
2   Mark Antony claims that he has not come to 'praise'
    Caesar (line 2). What impression of Caesar's character
    does he build up here, however? *How* does he do this?
3   What impression of himself does Mark Antony seek to cre-
    ate? How successful is he?
4   What is the effect of the constant repetition of 'Brutus is an
    honourable man'?
5   Mark Antony exploits both the greed and the sentimental-
    ity of the crowd here. How?
6   What does this speech reveal to you about Mark Antony's
    character and skill as a politician?
7* Compare Mark Antony's funeral oration with the oration
    spoken by Brutus earlier in the same scene. What differ-

ences between the two men are revealed by their separate speeches?

8* Analyse Antony's words and behaviour in the rest of this scene (Act 3, Scene 2). To what extent does this confirm your impression of him?

Assignment

If you are familiar with Shakespeare's *Hamlet* (1601), reread carefully the soliloquies spoken by Hamlet himself. What light do they throw on his character and motives?

33

3 Creating conflict
Drama in action

At the heart of all drama is conflict: the clash of opposing forces. Sometimes this clash may be between the individual and his or her circumstances. The conflict that is dramatised in *Riders to the Sea*, for example (see pages 9–11) is between the loves and needs of the human world and the cruel forces of fate, represented by the hostile sea. At the close of the play, this conflict is resolved when Maurya (the old woman) is able to accept her destiny with resignation and calm. More usually, however, the clash that takes place arises because of differences in personalities. A character may be asked or expected to behave in a way that is at odds with his or her own nature. Alternatively, two or more characters of contrasting temperaments or aims may find themselves in opposition to each other. In approaching play extracts that focus on conflict, a reader needs to consider carefully the nature and *causes* of the conflict, as well as the dramatic form that it takes.

This section will concentrate on examining conflicts between individuals – both conflicts of will and conflicts of interest. Three types of human relationship will be analysed: the relationships between parent and child, between husband and wife, and between friend and friend.

Parent and child

Here is one of the most famous father/daughter conflicts of all. It takes place in the first scene of Shakespeare's *King Lear*, and involves a bitter disagreement between King Lear and his youngest daughter, Cordelia. Goneril and Regan (who are married to Albany and Cornwall respectively) are Cordelia's elder sisters. The King of France and the Duke of Burgundy are two suitors who have come to the court to seek Cordelia's hand in marriage. Read this extract carefully, and then consider the questions printed below it.

King Lear

Sennet. Enter one bearing a coronet, KING LEAR, CORNWALL, ALBANY, GONERIL, REGAN, CORDELIA, *and Attendants.*

LEAR

Attend the Lords of France and Burgundy, Gloucester.

GLOUCESTER

I shall, my Liege.

Exeunt Gloucester and Edmund

LEAR

Meantime, we shall express our darker purpose.
Give me the map there. Know that we have divided
In three our kingdom; and 'tis our fast intent
To shake all cares and business from our age,
Conferring them on younger strengths, while we
Unburthen'd crawl toward death. Our son of
     Cornwall,
And you, our no less loving son of Albany,
We have this hour a constant will to publish   10
Our daughters' several dowers, that future strife
May be prevented now. The Princes, France and
     Burgundy,
Great rivals in our youngest daughter's love,
Long in our court have made their amorous sojourn,
And here are to be answer'd. Tell me, my daughters,
(Since now we will divest us both of rule,
Interest of territory, cares of state)
Which of you shall we say doth love us most?
That we our largest bounty may extend

35

Where nature doth with merit challenge. Goneril,   20
Our eldest-born, speak first.

GONERIL

Sir, I love you more than word can wield the matter;
Dearer than eye-sight, space and liberty;
Beyond what can be valued rich or rare;
No less than life, with grace, health, beauty, honour;
As much as child e'er lov'd, or father found;
A love that makes breath poor and speech unable;
Beyond all manner of so much I love you.

CORDELIA (*Aside*)

What shall Cordelia speak? Love, and be silent.

LEAR

Of all these bounds, even from this line to this,   30
With shadowy forests and with champains rich'd,
With plenteous rivers and wide-skirted meads,
We make thee lady: to thine and Albany's issues
Be this perpetual. What says our second daughter
Our dearest Regan, wife of Cornwall?

REGAN

I am made of that self metal as my sister,
And prize me at her worth. In my true heart
I find she names my very deed of love;
Only she comes too short: that I profess
Myself an enemy to all other joys   40
Which the most precious square of sense possesses,
And find I am alone felicitate
In your dear highness' love.

CORDELIA (*Aside*)

               Then poor Cordelia!
Any yet not so; since I am sure my love's
More ponderous than my tongue.

LEAR

To thee and thine, hereditary ever,
Remain this ample third of our fair kingdom,
No less in space, validity, and pleasure,
Than that conferr'd on Goneril. Now, our joy,
Although our last, and least; to whose young love   50
The vines of France and milk of Burgundy
Strive to be interess'd; what can you say to draw
A third more opulent than your sisters? Speak.

CORDELIA

Nothing, my lord.

LEAR

Nothing?

CORDELIA

Nothing.

LEAR

Nothing will come of nothing: speak again.

CORDELIA

Unhappy that I am, I cannot heave
My heart into my mouth: I love your Majesty
According to my bond; no more nor less.   60

LEAR

How, how, Cordelia! Mend your speech a little,
Lest you may mar your fortunes.

CORDELIA

                    Good my Lord,
You have begot me, bred me, lov'd me: I
Return those duties back as are right fit,
Obey you, love you, and most honour you.
Why have my sisters husbands, if they say
They love you all? Happily, when I shall wed,
That lord whose hand must take my plight shall carry

37

Half my love with him, half my care and duty:
Sure I shall never marry like my sisters,
To love my father all.   70

LEAR

But goes thy heart with this?

CORDELIA

                                        Ay, my good Lord.

LEAR

So young, and so untender?

CORDELIA

So young, my Lord, and true.

LEAR

Let it be so; thy truth then be thy dower:
For, by the sacred radiance of the sun,
The mysteries of Hecate and the night,
By all the operation of the orbs
From whom we do exist and cease to be,
Here I disclaim all my paternal care,   80
Propinquity and property of blood,
And as a stranger to my heart and me
Hold thee from this for ever. The barbarous Scythian,
Or he that makes his generation messes
To gorge his appetite, shall to my bosom
Be as well neighbour'd, pitied, and reliev'd,
As thou my sometime daughter.

                                        William Shakespeare (1606)

1   What has King Lear decided to do with his kingdom?
    What reasons does he give for this decision?
2   What does he ask his daughters to do at lines 15–20? Why
    do you think he makes this demand? Do you consider it
    wise of him?

3 What do you imagine that Cordelia is feeling as she speaks her two 'asides' (lines 29 and 43)?
4 Why does Cordelia say, 'Nothing, my lord' (line 54)?
5 What is King Lear's response to this? Why do you think he reacts so violently?
6 Do you think Cordelia should have behaved differently? Give your reasons.
7* What parallel parent/child conflict is to be found in the sub-plot of *King Lear*?
8* How are the conflicts in *King Lear* resolved?

Husband and wife

The conflict illustrated above is essentially a conflict of wills, and it is perhaps interesting also to notice that King Lear and Cordelia have a great deal *in common* (such as their stubbornness!) as well as a number of differences. In the next passage, however, although the conflict between the characters is partly a result of the differences between their personalities, it is also a result of their different aims: the husband wishes to die an honourable death, the wife wants him to live.

The extract is taken from *A Man For All Seasons* by Robert Bolt. The play is set in Tudor England. Sir Thomas More, a devout Catholic, has been imprisoned in the Tower of London for refusing to accept the divorce of King Henry VIII from Queen Catherine of Aragon, or King Henry's position as Head of the newly created Church of England. He is awaiting trial for high treason, for which the sentence is death. He is being visited (for the last time) by his wife Alice, his daughter Margaret, and her husband Will Roper.

A Man for All Seasons

Enter JAILER.

JAILER Two minutes to go, sir. I thought you'd like to know.

MORE Two minutes!

JAILER Till seven o'clock, sir. Sorry. Two minutes.

Exit JAILER.

MORE Jailer—! (*Seizes* ROPER *by the arm.*) Will – go to him, talk to him, keep him occupied— (*Propelling him after* JAILER.)

ROPER How, sir?

MORE Anyhow! – Have you got any money?

ROPER (*eager*) Yes!

MORE No, don't try and bribe him! Let him play for it; he's got a pair of dice. And talk to him, you understand! And take this (*the wine*) – and mind you share it – do it properly, Will! (ROPER *nods vigorously and exits.*) Now listen, you must leave the country. All of you must leave the country.

MARGARET And leave you here?

MORE It makes no difference, Meg; they won't let you see me again. (*Breathlessly, a prepared speech under pressure.*) You must all go on the same day, but not on the same boat; different boats from different ports—

MARGARET After the trial, then.

MORE There'll be no trial, they have no case. Do this for me I beseech you?

MARGARET Yes.

MORE Alice? (*She turns her back.*) Alice, I command it!

ALICE (*harshly*) Right!

MORE (*looks into basket*) Oh, this is splendid; I know who packed this.

ALICE (*harshly*) I packed it.

10

20

MORE   Yes. (*Eats a morsel.*) You still make superlative   30
custard, Alice.

ALICE   Do I?

MORE   That's a nice dress you have on.

ALICE   It's my cooking dress.

MORE   It's very nice anyway. Nice colour.

ALICE   (*turns. Quietly*)   By God, you think very little of me.
(*Mounting bitterness.*) I know I'm a fool. But I'm no such
fool as at this time to be lamenting for my dresses! Or
to relish complimenting on my custard!

MORE   (*regarding her with frozen attention. He nods once or
twice*)   I am well rebuked. (*Holds out his hands.*) Al—!   40

ALICE   No! (*She remains where she is, glaring at him.*)

MORE   (*he is in great fear of her*)   I am faint when I think of
the worst that they may do to me. But worse than that
would be to go, with you not understanding why I go.

ALICE   I don't!

MORE   (*just hanging on to his self-possession*)   Alice, if you
can tell me that you understand, I think I can make a
good death, if I have to.

ALICE   Your death's no 'good' to me!

MORE   Alice, you must tell me that you understand!   50

ALICE   I don't! (*She throws it straight at his head.*) I don't
believe this had to happen.

MORE   (*his face is drawn*)   If you say that, Alice, I don't see
how I'm to face it.

ALICE   It's the truth!

MORE   (*gasping*)   You're an honest woman.

ALICE   Much good may it do me! I'll tell you what I'm
afraid of; that when you've gone, I shall hate you for it.

MORE   (*turns from her: his face working*)   Well, you mustn't,
Alice, that's all. (*Swiftly she crosses the stage to him; he*   60
turns and they clasp each other fiercely.) You mustn't, you—

ALICE   (*covers his mouth with her hand*)   S-s-sh. . . . As
for understanding, I understand you're the best man
that I ever met or am likely to; and if you go – well

41

God knows why I suppose – though as God's my witness God's kept deadly quiet about it! And if anyone
wants my opinion of the King and his Council they've
only to ask for it!

MORE Why, it's a lion I married! A lion! A lion! (*He*   70
breaks away from her face shining.) Get them to take half
this to Bishop Fisher – they've got him in the upper
gallery—

ALICE It's for you, not Bishop Fisher!

MORE Now do as I ask— (*Breaks off a piece of the custard
and eats it.*) Oh, it's good, it's very, very good. (*He puts
his face in his hands;* ALICE *and* MARGARET *comfort him;*
ROPER *and* JAILER *erupt on to the stage above, wrangling
fiercely.*)

JAILER It's no good, sir! I know what you're up to! And
it can't be done!

ROPER Another minute, man!

JAILER (*to* MORE *descending*) Sorry, sir, time's up!

ROPER (*gripping his shoulder from behind*) For pity's   80
sake—!

JAILER (*shaking him off*) Now don't do that, sir! Sir
Thomas, the ladies will have to go now!

MORE You said seven o'clock!

JAILER It's seven now. You must understand my position, sir.

MORE But one more minute!

MARGARET Only a little while – give us a little while!

JAILER (*reproving*) Now, Miss, you don't want to get me
into trouble.   90

ALICE Do as you're gold. Be off at once!

*The first stroke of seven is heard on a heavy, deliberate bell, which
continues, reducing what follows to a babble.*

JAILER (*taking* MARGARET *firmly by the upper arm*) Now
come along, Miss; you'll get your father into trouble as
well as me. (ROPER *descends and grabs him.*) Are you ob-

structing me, sir? (MARGARET *embraces* MORE, *and dashes up the stairs and exits, followed by* ROPER. *Taking* ALICE *gingerly by the arm.*) Now, my lady, no trouble!

ALICE (*throwing him off as she rises*) Don't put your muddy hand on me!

JAILER Am I to call the guard then? Then come on!

ALICE, *facing him, puts foot on bottom stair and so retreats before him, backwards.*

MORE For God's sake, man, we're saying good-bye!   100

JAILER You don't know what you're asking, sir. You don't know how you're watched.

ALICE Filthy, stinking, gutter-bred turnkey!

JAILER Call me what you like, ma'am; you've got to go.

ALICE I'll see you suffer for this!

JAILER You're doing your husband no good!

MORE Alice, good-bye, my love!

On this, the last stroke of the seven sounds. ALICE *raises her hand, turns, and with considerable dignity, exits.*

     Robert Bolt (Heinemann Educational Books, 1960)

1 What does More's refusal to bribe the jailer show about his character?
2 Why does Alice resent More's compliments about her cooking and her dress? Do you sympathise with her?
3 What makes the conflict in this extract 'dramatic'?
4 How is the conflict resolved?
5 What is your impression from this scene of the relationship between husband and wife?

In the passage above, husband and wife were able to make peace with each other. In the next extract, from *Edward II* by Christopher Marlowe, the conflict of interests seems too extreme for a resolution to be possible. King Edward is rejecting his wife Isabella, because of his homosexual love for his friend Gaveston. The passage opens with the news that Gaveston has been exiled.

Edward II

GAVESTON

My lord, I hear it whisper'd everywhere,
That I am banish'd and must fly the land.

KING EDWARD

'Tis true, sweet Gaveston: O, were it false!
The legate of the Pope will have it so,
And thou must hence, or I shall be depos'd.
But I will reign to be reveng'd of them;
And therefore, sweet friend, take it patiently.
Live where thou wilt, I'll send thee gold enough;
And long thou shalt not stay, or, if thou dost,
I'll come to thee; my love shall ne'er decline.   10

GAVESTON

Is all my hope turn'd to this hell of grief?

KING EDWARD

Rend not my heart with thy too-piercing words.
Thou from this land, I from myself am banish'd.

GAVESTON

To go from hence grieves not poor Gaveston;
But to forsake you, in whose gracious looks
The blessedness of Gaveston remains;
For nowhere else seeks he felicity.

KING EDWARD

And only this torments my wretched soul,
That, whether I will or no, thou must depart.
Be Governor of Ireland in my stead,   20

And there abide till fortune call thee home.
Here, take my picture, and let me wear thine:

They exchange pictures.

O, might I keep thee here, as I do this,
Happy were I! but now most miserable.

GAVESTON

'Tis something to be pitied of a king.

KING EDWARD

Thou shalt not hence; I'll hide thee, Gaveston.

GAVESTON

I shall be found, and then 'twill grieve me more.

KING EDWARD

Kind words and mutual talk makes our grief greater:
Therefore, with dumb embracement, let us part.
Stay, Gaveston; I cannot leave thee thus.   30

GAVESTON

For every look, my lord, drops down a tear.
Seeing I must go, do not renew my sorrow.

KING EDWARD

The time is little that thou hast to stay,
And, therefore, give me leave to look my fill.
But, come, sweet friend; I'll bear thee on thy way.

GAVESTON

The peers will frown.

KING EDWARD

I pass not for their anger. Come, let's go:
O, that we might as well return as go!

Enter QUEEN ISABELLA

QUEEN ISABELLA

Whither goes my lord?

KING EDWARD

    Fawn not on me, French strumpet; get thee gone!   40

QUEEN ISABELLA

    On whom but on my husband should I fawn?

GAVESTON

    On Mortimer; with whom, ungentle queen, –
    I say no more – judge you the rest, my lord.

QUEEN ISABELLA

    In saying this, thou wrong'st me, Gaveston.
    Is't not enough that thou corrupt'st my lord,
    And art a bawd to his affections,
    But thou must call mine honour thus in question?

GAVESTON

    I mean not so; your grace must pardon me.

KING EDWARD

    Thou art too familiar with that Mortimer,
    And by thy means is Gaveston exil'd.   50
    But I would wish thee reconcile the lords,
    Or thou shalt ne'er be reconcil'd to me.

QUEEN ISABELLA

    Your highness knows, it lies not in my power.

KING EDWARD

    Away, then! touch me not. – Come, Gaveston.

QUEEN ISABELLA

    Villain, 'tis thou that robb'st me of my lord.

GAVESTON

    Madam, 'tis you that rob me of my lord.

KING EDWARD

    Speak not unto her: let her droop and pine.

QUEEN ISABELLA

 Wherein, my lord, have I deserv'd these words?
 Witness the tears that Isabella sheds.
 Witness this heart, that, sighing for thee, breaks, 60
 How dear my lord is to poor Isabel!

KING EDWARD

 And witness heaven how dear thou art to me.
 There weep; for, till my Gaveston be repeal'd,
 Assure thyself thou com'st not in my sight.

     Exeunt KING EDWARD *and* GAVESTON.

QUEEN ISABELLA

 O miserable and distressed queen!
 Would, when I left sweet France, and was embarked,
 That charming Circe, walking on the waves,
 Had chang'd my shape! or at the marriage-day
 The cup of Hymen had been full of poison!
 Or with those arms, that twin'd about my neck, 70
 I had been stifled, and not liv'd to see
 The king my lord thus abandon me!
 Like frantic Juno will I fill the earth
 With ghastly murmur of my sighs and cries;
 For never doted Jove on Ganymede
 So much as he on cursed Gaveston.
 But that will more exasperate his wrath;
 I must entreat him, I must speak him fair,
 And be a means to call home Gaveston.
 And yet he'll ever dote on Gaveston; 80
 And so am I for ever miserable.

       Christopher Marlowe (1592)

1 What do you learn about the nature of Edward's and
 Gaveston's relationship in the section before Isabella's
 entrance?

2 Discuss Edward's attitude towards Isabella in this extract. Do you consider his behaviour here reasonable?
3 In what ways are the tensions between Gaveston and Isabella revealed in this extract?
4 To what extent do you feel sympathy for Isabella here? What is the effect of her soliloquy (lines 65–81)?

Friend and friend

Not all conflicts, of course, contain the seriousness and potential for tragedy of the three previous extracts. Conflict may, after all, be primarily humorous in effect. As an illustration of this, read the following two extracts carefully. Both of them focus on an essentially similar situation: an argument between two women who believe they are in love with the same man. The first extract is from Act 3 Scene 2 of Shakespeare's *A Midsummer Night's Dream*. The second extract is from *The Importance of Being Earnest* by Oscar Wilde.

A Midsummer Night's Dream

HERMIA

O me! you juggler! you canker-blossom!
You thief of love! what! have you come by night
And stol'n my love's heart from him?

HELENA

Fine, i'faith!
Have you no modesty, no maiden shame,
No touch of bashfulness? What! will you tear
Impatient answers from my gentle tongue?
Fie, fie! You counterfeit, you puppet you!

HERMIA

Puppet! why, so: ay, that way goes the game.

Now I perceive that she hath made compare
Between our statures: she hath urg'd her height;   10
And with her personage, her tall personage,
Her height, forsooth, she hath prevail'd with him.
And are you grown so high in his esteem,
Because I am so dwarfish and so low?
How low am I, thou painted maypole? speak;
How low am I? I am not yet so low
But that my nails can reach unto thine eyes.

HELENA

I pray you, though you mock me, gentlemen,
Let her not hurt me: I was never curst;
I have no gift at all in shrewishness;   20
I am a right maid for my cowardice:
Let her not strike me. You perhaps may think,
Because she is something lower than myself,
That I can match her.

HERMIA

                Lower! hark, again!
                William Shakespeare (1596)

The Importance of Being Earnest

CECILY (*rather shy and confidingly*) Dearest Gwendolen,
there is no reason why I should make a secret of it to
you. Our little county newspaper is sure to chronicle
the fact next week. Mr Ernest Worthing and I are engaged to be married.

GWENDOLEN (*quite politely, rising and moving to centre*) My
darling Cecily, I think there must be some slight error.
Mr Ernest Worthing is engaged to me. The announce-
ment will appear in the *Morning Post* on Saturday at the
latest.   10

CECILY (*very politely, rising and moving to right centre*) I am afraid you must be under some misconception. Ernest proposed to me exactly ten minutes ago. (*She shows her diary*)

GWENDOLEN (*examining the diary carefully through her lorgnette*) It is certainly very curious, for he asked *me* to be his wife yesterday afternoon at five-thirty. If you would care to verify the incident, pray do so. I never travel without my diary. (*She produces a diary of her own*) One should always have something sensational to read in the train. I am so sorry, dear Cecily, if it is any disappointment to you, but I am afraid *I* have the prior claim. 20

CECILY It would distress me more than I can tell you, dear Gwendolen, if it caused you any mental or physical anguish, but I feel bound to point out that since Ernest proposed to *you* he clearly has changed his mind.

GWENDOLEN (*meditatively*) If the poor fellow has been entrapped into any foolish promise I shall consider it my duty to rescue him *at once*, and with a *firm hand*.

CECILY (*thoughtfully and sadly, moving slowly right*) Whatever unfortunate entanglement my dear boy may have got into, *I* will never reproach him with it *after* we are married. 30

GWENDOLEN Do you allude to *me*, Miss Cardew, as an entanglement? You are presumptuous. On an occasion of this kind it becomes more than a moral duty to speak one's mind. It becomes a pleasure.

CECILY (*moving back to right centre*) Do you suggest, Miss Fairfax, that I entrapped Ernest into an engagement? How dare you? This is no time for wearing the shallow mask of manners. When I see a *spade* I call it a *spade*. 40

GWENDOLEN (*satirically, up left centre*) I am glad to say that I have never seen a spade. It is obvious that our social spheres have been *widely* different.

Oscar Wilde (1895)

1 Compare the different types of insult that the two pairs of women hurl at each other.
2 What changes in tone do you notice in the course of these two quarrels?
3 What seem to you the main differences between the two arguments? Look especially at the types of *language* used by the characters.
4 Which argument do you find the more entertaining, and why?
5 Do you consider that either argument is convincingly *won*?

Assignment

Read *Travesties* (1975) by Tom Stoppard. What conflicts are explored in this play between (a) different sets of beliefs, and (b) different types of personality?

4   Using the theatre Stage and page

The previous two chapters have tended to focus on the *spoken* word. Chapter 2 looked at the different types of language in which characters might express themselves, and at the significance of what they say and to whom they are speaking. Chapter 3 looked more closely at the ways in which characters' words can be affected by their feelings and by the particular situations in which they find themselves, and also considered the ways in which conflicts between characters can be represented verbally. In this chapter, however, discussion will be centred not only on what is said and by whom, but also on *where* and *when* it is said. For ultimately, after all, most plays are intended for performance.

Inevitably, a playwright's work exists most powerfully and completely on stage rather than page, for on a stage it is possible to control an audience's attention and interest by vision as well as by sound (and also by a whole range of different *kinds* of sounds). Using the physical world of the theatre as an active force that can counterpoint the developing concerns of a play and its characters is therefore a very important part of the special skill of a dramatist. And it is a part that a reader (rather than watcher) of a play must be especially careful not to underestimate. The aim of this section, then, is to highlight some of the ways in which the possibilities offered by *external* factors – such as stage-sets, lighting, sound effects and props – may be exploited for dramatic effect.

Set

Below is an introductory example of how a stage set may suggest or reinforce the themes of a play. It is taken from *Death of a Salesman* by the American playwright Arthur Miller, and it describes the home of Willy Loman (the Salesman) who is the play's central character. Read the extract carefully, and then consider the questions that follow it. As in previous chapters, further questions (marked with asterisks) are offered for readers who are familiar with the whole play.

Death of a Salesman

A melody is heard, played upon a flute. It is small and fine, telling of grass and trees and the horizon. The curtain rises.

Before us is the SALESMAN'S *house. We are aware of towering, angular shapes behind it, surrounding it on all sides. Only the blue light of the sky falls upon the house and forestage; the surrounding area shows an angry glow of orange. As more light appears, we see a solid vault of apartment houses around the small, fragile-seeming home. An air of the dream clings to the place, a dream rising out of reality. The kitchen at centre seems actual enough, for there is a kitchen table with three chairs, and a refrigerator. But* 10
no other fixtures are seen. At the back of the kitchen there is a draped entrance, which leads to the living-room. To the right of the kitchen, on a level raised two feet, is a bedroom furnished only with a brass bedstead and a straight chair. On a shelf over the bed a silver athletic trophy stands. A window opens on to the apartment house at the side.

Behind the kitchen, on a level raised six and a half feet, is the boys' bedroom, at present barely visible. Two beds are dimly seen, and at the back of the room a dormer window. (This bedroom is above the unseen living-room.) At the left a stairway curves up to 20
it from the kitchen.

The entire setting is wholly or, in some places, partially transparent. The roof-line of the house is one-dimensional; under and over it we see the apartment buildings. Before the house lies an apron, curving beyond the forestage into the orchestra. This forward area serves as the back yard as well as the locale of all

*Willy's imaginings and of his city scenes. Whenever the action is
in the present the actors observe the imaginary wall-lines, entering
the house only through its door at the left. But in the scenes of the
past these boundaries are broken, and characters enter or leave a*   30
room by stepping 'through' a wall on to the forestage.

Arthur Miller (Penguin, 1949)

1   What do the general layout of this house and the kind of
    objects within it suggest to you about the people who live
    there?

2   Willy Loman lives in the city. How does Miller use staging
    and lighting to suggest an urban environment? What de-
    tails make the environment a threatening one?

3   *Death of a Salesman* suggests two alternatives to city life: the
    rural world, and the world of the imagination. How are
    these different possibilities represented by the play's set and
    sound effects?

4* Explain the significance · of the comment 'An air of the
    dream clings to the place' (line 8).

5* What is the special importance of the refrigerator (line 10)
    and the silver athletic trophy (line 15)?

6* The original title for *Death of a Salesman* was 'The Inside of
    His Head', and Miller said that his first idea for a set was a
    vision of a man's head opening up so that we could see
    what went on inside. To what extent does this set still
    achieve that purpose? Do you find it more or less effective
    than the original idea?

In *Death of a Salesman*, although an individual acting area
may be used to represent several different times or places, the basic
set remains unchanged throughout the play – just as Willy
Loman himself remains imprisoned within his own fixed set
of ideas and beliefs. In the following sequence of extracts, however – taken from *The Royal Hunt of the Sun* by Peter Shaffer –
the basic set can be seen to alter as the action progresses. In

this way, Shaffer is able not only to represent the conflicting attitudes to life of two different groups of characters, but also to suggest in a *visual* way the symbolic significance of certain actions.

The Royal Hunt of the Sun describes the expedition in the sixteenth century of Spanish conquistadors to the dazzlingly rich and beautiful kingdom of the Incas in Peru. In theory, their purpose is to convert a heathen culture (the Incas worship the sun) to the Christian faith. In practice, their motives are much more mercenary. They are greedy for gold.

The play opens in Spain with the following set direction:

A bare stage. On the back wall, which is of wood, hangs a huge metal medallion, quartered by four black crucifixes, sharpened to resemble swords.

When the action moves to Peru, however, the set changes:

The stage darkens and the huge medallion high on the back wall begins to glow. Great cries of 'Inca!' are heard . . . Exotic music mixes with the chanting. Slowly the medallion opens outwards to form a huge golden sun, with twelve great rays. In the centre stands ATAHUALLPA, *sovereign Inca of Peru, masked, crowned, and dressed in gold.*

Consider the following questions briefly, before moving on to the longer passage:

1 What is the significance of the fact that the Spanish crucifixes are 'black' and 'sharpened'?
2 For what reasons is a 'huge golden sun' an appropriate symbol for the Inca kingdom?

The following extract (Act 2, Scene 6) portrays what Shaffer describes elsewhere as 'the desecration of Peru'. In an act of

55

treachery the Spaniards have massacred three thousand Incas and taken Atahuallpa (their ruler) captive. They promise his release if the Incas fill all of the chamber with gold. Old Martin is the narrator, telling his story many years after the events, and all of the other named characters are also Spaniards. Cuzco (line 35) is the Inca capital.

The Royal Hunt of the Sun

Enter OLD MARTIN

OLD MARTIN Slowly the pile increased. The army waited nervously and licked its lips. Greed began to rise in us like a tide of sea.

A music of bells and humming.

THE SECOND GOLD PROCESSION
and THE RAPE OF THE SUN.

Another line of Indian porters comes in, bearing gold objects. Like the first, this instalment of treasure is guarded by Spanish soldiers, but they are less disciplined now. Two of them assault an Indian and grab his headdress. Another snatches a necklace at sword's point.

Above, in the chamber, the treasure is piled up as before. DIEGO *and the* CHAVEZ *brothers are seen supervising. They begin to explore the sun itself, leaning out of the chamber and prodding at the petals with their halberds. Suddenly* DIEGO *gives a cry of triumph, drives his halberd into a slot in one of the rays, and pulls out the gold inlay. The sun gives a deep groan, like the sound of a great animal being wounded. With greedy yelps, all the soldiers below rush at the sun and start pulling it to bits; they tear out the gold inlays and fling them on the ground, while terrible groans fill the air. In a moment only the great gold frame remains; a broken, blackened sun.*

Enter DE SOTO

DIEGO Welcome back, sir.

DE SOTO Diego, it's good to see you.

DIEGO What's it like, sir? Is there trouble?

DE SOTO It's grave quiet. Terrible. Men just standing in
fields for hundreds of miles. Waiting for their God to
come back to them.

DIEGO Well, if he does they'll be fighters again and we're   10
for the limepit.

DE SOTO How's the General?

DIEGO An altered man. No one's ever seen him so easy.
He spends hours each day with the King. He's going to
find it hard when he has to do it.

DE SOTO Do what?

DIEGO Kill him, sir.

DE SOTO He can't do that. Not after a contract wit-
nessed before a whole army.

DIEGO Well, he can't let him go, that's for certain . . .   20
Never mind, he'll find a way. He's as cunning as the
devil's grandad, save your pardon, sir.

DE SOTO No, you're right, boy.

DIEGO Tell us about their capital, then. What's it like?

*During the preceding, a line of Indians, bent double, has been
loaded with the torn-off petals from the sun. Now, as* DE SOTO
*describes Cuzco, they file slowly round the stage and go off, stag-
gering under the weight of the great gold slabs. When he reaches
the account of the garden, the marvellous objects he tells of appear
in the treasure chamber above, borne by Indians, and are stacked
up until they fill it completely. The interior of the sun is now a
solid mass of gold.*

DE SOTO Completely round. They call it the navel of the
earth and that's what it looks like. In the middle was a
huge temple, the centre of their faith. The walls were
plated with gold, enough to blind us. Inside, set out on

tables, golden platters for the sun to dine off. Outside, the garden: acres of gold soil planted with gold maize. Entire apple trees in gold. Gold birds on the branches. Gold geese and ducks. Gold butterflies in the air on silver strings. And – imagine this – away in a field, life-size, twenty golden llamas grazing with their kids. The garden of the Sun at Cuzco. A wonder of the earth. Look at it now.

DIEGO (*rushing in below*) Hey! The room's full!

DOMINGO It isn't!

SALINAS It is. Look!

JUAN He's right. It's full!

DIEGO We can start the share-out now. (*Cheers*)

PEDRO What'll you do with your lot, Juan, boy?

JUAN Buy a farm.

PEDRO Me, too. I don't work for nobody ever again.

DOMINGO Ah, you can buy a palace, easy, with a share of that. Never mind a pissing farm! What d'you say, Diego?

DIEGO Oh, I want a farm, A good stud farm, and a stable of Arabs, just for me to ride! What will you have, Salinas?

SALINAS Me? A bash-house! (*Laughter*) Right in the middle of Trujillo, open six to six, filled with saddle-backed fillies from Andalusia . . .

Enter VASCA *rolling a huge gold sun, like a hoop.*

VASCA Look what I got, boys! The sun! He ain't public any more, the old sun. He's private property!

DOMINGO There's no private property, till share out.

VASCA Well, here's the exception. I risked my life to get this a hundred feet up.

JUAN Dungballs!

VASCA I did! Off the temple roof.

PEDRO Come on, boy, get it up there with the rest.

VASCA No. Finding's keepings. That's the law.

JUAN   What law?

VASCA   My law. Do you think you'll see any of this once
the share-out starts? Not on your pissing life. You leave
it up there, boy, you won't see nothing again.

PEDRO   (*to his brother*)   He's right there.

JUAN   Do you think so?

VASCA   Of course. Officers first, then the Church. You'll
get pissing nothing. (*A pause*)   70

SALINAS   So let's have a share-out now, then!

DOMINGO   Why not? We're all entitled.

VASCA   Of course we are.

JUAN   All right. I'm with you.

PEDRO   Good boy!

SALINAS   Come on, then.

They all make a rush for the Sun Chamber.

DE SOTO   Where do you think you're going? . . . You
know the General's orders. Nothing till share-out.
Penalty for breach, death. Disperse now. I'll go and see
the General.   80

They hesitate.

(*Quietly*) Get to your posts.

Reluctantly, they disperse.

And keep a sharp watch. The danger's not over yet.

DIEGO   I'd say it had only just begun, sir.

He goes. DE SOTO *remains.*

Peter Shaffer (Longman, 1964)

1   Why do you think Shaffer describes what happens in the
long stage direction as the 'rape' of the sun? What sound
effects contribute to this impression?

2   The sun is described as 'broken' and 'blackened'. What is
the significance of this?

3   What differences between Spanish and Inca attitudes are
exposed in this scene? Where do your sympathies lie?

Lighting

In *The Royal Hunt of the Sun*, the sun is represented not only by a golden medallion but also by lighting effects. In this way, the continued might and majesty of the Inca kingdom is suggested to us by the circles of light that still pour from the sun, even when Peru and its ruler have been violated. At the close of the play, for example, Atahuallpa is brutally murdered by the Spanish, despite their promise to free him in return for gold. Yet the light of the sun still survives, to irradiate his dead body:

Slowly, in semi-darkness, the stage fills with all the Indians, robed in black and terracotta, wearing the great golden funeral masks of ancient Peru. Grouped round the prone body, they intone a strange Chant of Resurrection, punctuated by hollow beats on the drums and by long, long silences in which they turn their immense triangular eyes enquiringly up to the sky. Finally, after three great cries appear to summon it, the sun rises. Its rays fall on the body.

Another twentieth-century play that uses effects of light and dark in a symbolic way is *The Birthday Party* by Harold Pinter. It is a highly unusual play, focusing on a nervous and with-drawn man called Stanley who lives in a seedy seaside board-ing house with his landlady, Meg Boles, and her husband, Petey. Lulu is the young woman from next door. Two sinister strangers, Goldberg and McCann, have arrived at the board-ing house apparently in search of Stanley. The play traces the way in which their presence menaces and disrupts his whole existence. This extract (from the end of Act 2) describes the bizarre happenings at the 'birthday party' Meg insists on giv-ing in Stanley's honour. The toy drum which features in the action was her present to him.

Read this passage carefully, and then look closely at the questions which follow.

The Birthday Party

MEG (*rising*) I want to play a game!

GOLDBERG A game?

LULU What game?

MEG Any game.

LULU (*jumping up*) Yes, let's play a game.

GOLDBERG What game?

MCCANN Hide and seek.

LULU Blind man's buff.

MEG Yes!

GOLDBERG You want to play blind man's buff? 10

LULU and MEG Yes!

GOLDBERG All right. Blind man's buff. Come on! Everyone up! (*Rising*.) McCann. Stanley – Stanley!

MEG Stanley. Up.

GOLDBERG What's the matter with him?

MEG (*bending over him*) Stanley, we're going to play a
game. Oh, come on, don't be sulky, Stan.

LULU Come on.

STANLEY *rises*. MCCANN *rises*.

GOLDBERG Right! Now – who's going to be blind first?

LULU Mrs Boles. 20

MEG Not me.

GOLDBERG Of course you.

MEG Who, me?

LULU (*taking her scarf from her neck*) Here you are.

MCCANN How do you play this game?

LULU (*tying her scarf round* MEG's *eyes*) Haven't you ever
played blind man's buff? Keep still, Mrs Boles. You
mustn't be touched. But you can't move after she's
blind. You must stay where you are after she's blind.
And if she touches you then you become blind. Turn 30
round. How many fingers am I holding up?

MEG I can't see.

LULU   Right.

GOLDBERG   Right! Everyone move about. McCann. Stanley. Now stop. Now still. Off you go!

STANLEY *is downstage, right,* MEG *moves about the room.*
GOLDBERG *fondles* LULU *at arm's length.* MEG *touches* MCCANN.

MEG   Caught you!

LULU   Take off your scarf.

MEG   What lovely hair!

LULU   *(untying the scarf)*   There.

MEG   It's you!   40

GOLDBERG   Put it on, McCann.

LULU   *(tying it on* MCCANN*)*   There. Turn round. How many fingers am I holding up?

MEG   I don't know.

GOLDBERG   Right! Everyone move about. Right. Stop! Still!

MCCANN *begins to move.*

MEG   Oh, this is lovely!

GOLDBERG   Quiet! Tch, tch, tch. Now – all move again. Stop! Still!

MCCANN *moves about.* GOLDBERG *fondles* LULU *at arm's length.*
MACCANN *draws near* STANLEY. *He stretches his arm and touches*
STANLEY'S *glasses.*

MEG   It's Stanley!   50

GOLDBERG   *(to* LULU*)*   Enjoying the game?

MEG   It's your turn, Stan.

MCCANN *takes off the scarf.*

MCCANN   *(to* STANLEY*)*   I'll take your glasses.

MCCANN *takes* STANLEY'S *glasses.*

MEG   Give me the scarf.

GOLDBERG   *(holding* LULU*)*   Tie his scarf, Mrs Boles.

MEG   That's what I'm doing. (*To* STANLEY.) Can you see my nose?

GOLDBERG   He can't. Ready? Right! Everyone move. Stop! And still!

STANLEY *stands blindfold.* MCCANN *backs slowly across the stage to the left. He breaks* STANLEY'S *glasses, snapping the frames.* MEG *is downstage, left,* LULU *and* GOLDBERG *upstage centre, close together.* STANLEY *begins to move, very slowly, across the stage to the left.* MCCANN *picks up the drum and places it sideways in* STANLEY'S *path.* STANLEY *walks into the drum and falls over with his foot caught in it.*

MEG   Ooh!   60

GOLDBERG   Sssh!

STANLEY *rises. He begins to move towards* MEG, *dragging the drum on his foot. He reaches her and stops. His hands move towards her and they reach her throat. He begins to strangle her.* MCCANN *and* GOLDBERG *rush forward and throw him off.*

BLACKOUT

There is now no light at all through the window. The stage is in darkness.

LULU   The lights!

GOLDBERG   What's happened?

LULU   The lights!

MCCANN   Wait a minute.

GOLDBERG   Where is he?

MCCANN   Let go of me!

GOLDBERG   Who's this?

LULU   Someone's touching me!

MCCANN   Where is he?   70

MEG   Why has the light gone out?

GOLDBERG   Where's your torch? (MCCANN *shines the torch in* GOLDBERG'S *face.*) Not on me! (MCCANN *shifts the torch. It is knocked from his hand and falls. It goes out.*)

63

MCCANN   My torch!

LULU   Oh God!

GOLDBERG   Where's your torch? Pick up your torch!

MCCANN   I can't find it.

LULU   Hold me. Hold me.

GOLDBERG   Get down on your knees. Help him find the torch.

LULU   I can't.

MCCANN   It's gone.

MEG   Why has the light gone out?

GOLDBERG   Everyone quiet! Help him find the torch.

80

Silence. Grunts from MCCANN *and* GOLDBERG *on their knees. Suddenly there is a sharp, sustained rat-a-tat with a stick on the side of the drum from the back of the room. Silence. Whimpers from* LULU.

GOLDBERG   Over here. McCann!

MCCANN   Here.

GOLDBERG   Come to me, come to me. Easy. Over there.

GOLDBERG *and* MCCANN *move up left of the table.* STANLEY *moves down right of the table.* LULU *suddenly perceives him moving towards her, screams and faints.* GOLDBERG *and* MCCANN *turn and stumble against each other.*

GOLDBERG   What is it?

MCCANN   Who's that?

GOLDBERG   What is it?

90

In the darkness STANLEY *picks up* LULU *and places her on the table.*

MEG   It's Lulu!

GOLDBERG *and* MCCANN *move downstage, right.*

GOLDBERG   Where is she?

MCCANN   She fell.

GOLDBERG   Where?

MCCANN   About here.

GOLDBERG   Help me pick her up.

MCCANN (*moving downstage, left*)   I can't find her.

GOLDBERG   She must be somewhere.

MCCANN   She's not here.

GOLDBERG (*moving downstage, left*)   She must be.   100

MCCANN   She's gone.

MCCANN *finds the torch on the floor, shines it on the table and* STANLEY. LULU *is lying spread-eagled on the table,* STANLEY *bent over her.* STANLEY, *as soon as the torchlight hits him, begins to giggle.* GOLDBERG *and* MCCANN *move towards him. He backs, giggling, the torch on his face. They follow him upstage, left. He backs against the hatch, giggling. The torch draws closer. His giggle rises and grows as he flattens himself against the wall. Their figures converge upon him.*

CURTAIN

Harold Pinter (Methuen, 1958)

1   In what ways is this scene made disturbing for an audience?

2   What do the various forms of darkness and blindness that are presented here seem to you to represent?

3   What is the dramatic effect of the torchlight shining on Stanley's face at the end of this scene?

4   If this stage-darkness is seen, in part, as a metaphor for Stanley's subconscious mind, what is the significance of his behaviour here towards women?

Sound effects

In the previous extract, the 'sharp, sustained rat-a-tat with a stick on the side of the drum' (between lines 84 and 85) gives an example of the way in which a dramatist may incorporate unnerving or unexplained sounds within the action of a play as a means of increasing dramatic tension.

Below is another – very famous – example, taken from Shakespeare's *Macbeth*. Macbeth, an eleventh-century Scottish noble, has been persuaded by his wife to murder Duncan (the King of Scotland, who is staying as a guest in their castle), in the hope of becoming king himself. This extract (Act 2, Scene 2) opens as Lady Macbeth awaits her husband's return from the royal bedchamber, where he has killed the sleeping King.

Macbeth

Enter LADY MACBETH

LADY MACBETH

That which hath made them drunk hath made me
   bold:
What hath quenched them hath given me fire. Hark!
   Peace!
It was the owl that shrieked, the fatal bellman,
Which gives the stern'st good-night. He is about it:
The doors are open; and the surfeited grooms
Do mock their charge with snores: I have drugged
   their possets,
That death and nature do contend about them,
Whether they live or die.

MACBETH (*Within*)

                    Who's there? what, ho!

LADY MACBETH

Alack! I am afraid they have awaked,
And 'tis not done: the attempt and not the deed   10
Confounds us. Hark! I laid their daggers ready;
He could not miss them. Had he not resembled
My father as he slept, I had done't.

Enter MACBETH.

                            My husband!

MACBETH
I have done the deed. Didst thou not hear a noise?

LADY MACBETH
I hear the owl scream and the crickets cry.
Did not you speak?

MACBETH
            When?

LADY MACBETH
              Now.

MACBETH
                    As I descended?

LADY MACBETH
Ay.

MACBETH
          Hark!
Who lies i' the second chamber?

LADY MACBETH
                       Donalbain.

MACBETH (*Looking at his hand*)
This is a sorry sight.   20

LADY MACBETH
A foolish thought to say a sorry sight.

MACBETH
There's one did laugh in's sleep, and one cried
   'Murder!'
That they did wake each other: I stood and heard
   them;

But they did say their prayers, and addressed them
Again to sleep.

LADY MACBETH

There are two lodged together.

MACBETH

One cried 'God bless us!' and 'Amen' the other:
As they had seen me with these hangman's hands.
Listening their fear, I could not say 'Amen'
When they did say 'God bless us!'

LADY MACBETH

Consider it not so deeply.

MACBETH

But wherefore could not I pronounce 'Amen'?   30
I had most need of blessing, and 'Amen'
Stuck in my throat.

LADY MACBETH

These deeds must not be thought
After these ways: so, it will make us mad.

MACBETH

Methought I heard a voice cry 'Sleep no more!
Macbeth does murder sleep' – the innocent sleep,
Sleep that knits up the ravelled sleave of care,
The death of each day's life, sore labour's bath,
Balm of hurt minds, great nature's second course,
Chief nourisher in life's feast, –

LADY MACBETH

What do you mean?

MACBETH

Still it cried 'Sleep no more!' to all the house: 40
'Glamis hath murdered sleep, and therefore Cawdor
Shall sleep no more – Macbeth shall sleep no more!'

LADY MACBETH

Who was it that thus cried? Why, worthy Thane,
You do unbend your noble strength to think
So brainsickly of things. Go get some water
And wash this filthy witness from your hand.
Why did you bring these daggers from the place?
They must lie there: go carry them, and smear
The sleepy grooms with blood.

MACBETH

I'll go no more:
I am afraid to think what I have done;   50
Look on't again I dare not.

LADY MACBETH

Infirm of purpose!
Give me the daggers. The sleeping and the dead
Are but as pictures; 'tis the eye of childhood
That fears a painted devil. If he do bleed,
I'll gild the faces of the grooms withal,
For it must seem their guilt.

Exit.

Knocking within

MACBETH

Whence is that knocking?
How is't with me, when every noise appals me?
What hands are here! Ha! they pluck out mine eyes.
Will all great Neptune's ocean wash this blood
Clean from my hand? No; this my hand will rather   60
The multitudinous seas incarnadine,
Making the green one red.

Re-enter LADY MACBETH

LADY MACBETH

My hands are of your colour; but I shame

To wear a heart so white. (*Knocking within.*) I hear a
   knocking
At the south entry; retire we to our chamber.
A little water clears us of this deed:
How easy is it then! Your constancy
Hath left you unattended. (*Knocking within.*) Hark!
   more knocking.
Get on your nightgown, lest occasion call us
And show us to be watchers. Be not lost   70
So poorly in your thoughts.

MACBETH

To know my deed, 'twere best not know myself.

Knocking within

Wake Duncan with thy knocking! I would thou
   couldst!

Exeunt

William Shakespeare (1606)

1   What noises does Lady Macbeth hear as she waits for Macbeth's return? How does she react to these sounds?
2   In what ways do the language and manner of the characters' first words to each other (lines 13–20) suggest their nervousness?
3   What thoughts are obsessing Macbeth throughout the rest of this scene, making him incapable of further action?
4   In what ways does Lady Macbeth take control of the situation here?
5   What is the effect of the knocking in this scene?
6   What does the last line suggest to you about Macbeth's state of mind?

Another form of sound effect that can create mood and atmosphere within a play is the use of music. The following extract –

again by Shakespeare – is taken from Act 1, Scene 2 of *The Tempest*. Prospero, the exiled Duke of Milan, is living with his daughter Miranda on a magical island, attended by fairy spirits such as Ariel. A shipwreck has washed ashore Prince Ferdinand, son of the King of Naples, who believes that his father has died in the storm. In this passage, Ariel's singing can not only be seen as something strange and beautiful, like the world of the enchanted island, but music itself is also shown to have the magical power to guide and control characters' lives.

The Tempest

Re-enter ARIEL, *invisible, playing and singing;* FERDINAND *following*
ARIEL'S SONG.
Come unto these yellow sands,
And then take hands:
Courtsied when you have and kiss'd
The wild waves whist:
Foot it featly here and there,
And sweet sprites bear
The burthen. Hark, hark.

(Burthen dispersedly.) *Bow-wow.*
The watch dogs bark:
(Burthen dispersedly.) *Bow-wow.* 10
Hark, hark! I hear
The strain of strutting chanticleer
Cry – (Burthen dispersedly.) *Cock a diddle dow.*

FERDINAND
Where should this music be? i' th' air or th'earth?
It sounds no more: and, sure, it waits upon
Some god o' th' island. Sitting on a bank,

71

Weeping again the King my father's wrack,
This music crept by me upon the waters,
Allaying both their fury and my passion
With its sweet air: thence I have follow'd it,   20
Or it hath drawn me rather. But 'tis gone.
No, it begins again.

ARIEL'S SONG.

Full fadom five thy father lies;
Of his bones are coral made;
Those are pearls that were his eyes:
Nothing of him that doth fade,
But doth suffer a sea-change
Into something rich and strange.
Sea-nymphs hourly ring his knell:

(Burthen:) *Ding-dong.*   30

Hark! now I hear them, – Ding-dong, bell.

FERDINAND

The ditty does remember my drown'd father.
This is no mortal business, nor no sound
That the earth owes: – I hear it now above me.

PROSPERO

The fringed curtains of thine eye advance,
And say what thou seest yond.

MIRANDA

What is't? a spirit?
Lord, how it looks about! Believe me, sir,
It carries a brave form. But 'tis a spirit.

PROSPERO

No, wench; it eats and sleeps and hath such senses
As we have, such. This gallant which thou seest   40
Was in the wrack; and, but he's something stain'd
With grief (that's beauty's canker) thou mightst call
    him

72

A goodly person: he hath lost his fellows,
And strays about to find 'em.

MIRANDA

                         I might call him
A thing divine; for nothing natural
I ever saw so noble.

                     William Shakespeare (1611)

1   What atmosphere is conjured up here by the form and imagery of Ariel's songs?
2   Explain Ferdinand's reactions to the music. Why has he followed it?
3   Imagine that you were directing this scene. How would you choose to present this music on stage?
4* What role is played by music in *The Tempest* as a whole?
5* Discuss the significance and effect of songs in any others of Shakespeare's plays that you know.

Props

Props (which is short for 'properties') are the physical objects that characters may need to use in a drama in order to carry out certain actions, and often both the items and the actions will be merely routine. But it is also possible in a play for props to come to stand for or to suggest particular ideas or attitudes. And in such cases, the way in which characters regard or handle specific objects can assume considerable dramatic importance.

The following passage is taken from *Pygmalion* by George Bernard Shaw. The play describes the relationship between Professor Henry Higgins, a speech expert, and Eliza Doolittle, a Cockney flower-girl. Higgins has made a bet with his friend Pickering that he can train her to speak so that she could pass as a lady. They have just returned from a triumphant evening.

Read the passage carefully, and then consider the questions below it.

Pygmalion

The Wimpole Street laboratory. Midnight. Nobody in the room. The clock on the mantelpiece strikes twelve. The fire is not alight: it is a summer night.

Presently HIGGINS *and* PICKERING *are heard on the stairs.*

HIGGINS (*calling down to Pickering*) I say, Pick: lock up, will you? I shan't be going out again.

PICKERING Right. Can Mrs Pearce go to bed? We dont want anything more, do we?

HIGGINS Lord, no!

ELIZA *opens the door and is seen on the lighted landing in all the finery in which she has just won* HIGGINS's *bet for him. She comes to the hearth, and switches on the electric lights there. She is tired: her pallor contrasts strongly with her dark eyes and hair; and her expression is almost tragic. She takes off her cloak; puts her fan and gloves on the piano; and sits down on the bench, brooding and silent.* HIGGINS, *in evening dress, with overcoat and hat, comes in, carrying a smoking jacket which he has picked up downstairs. He takes off the hat and overcoat; throws them carelessly on the newspaper stand; disposes of his coat in the same way; puts on the smoking jacket; and throws himself wearily into the easy-chair at the hearth.* PICKERING, *similarly attired, comes in. He also takes off his hat and overcoat, and is about to throw them on* HIGGINS's *when he hesitates.*

PICKERING I say: Mrs Pearce will row if we leave these things lying about in the drawing room.

HIGGINS Oh, chuck them over the bannisters into the
  hall. She'll find them there in the morning and put
  them away all right. She'll think we were drunk. 10
PICKERING We are, slightly. Are there any letters?
HIGGINS I didnt look. (PICKERING *takes the overcoats and
  hats and goes downstairs.* HIGGINS *begins half singing half
  yawning an air from 'La Fanciulla del Golden West'. Suddenly
  he stops and exclaims*) I wonder where the devil my slippers are!

Eliza looks at him darkly; then rises suddenly and leaves the room.
HIGGINS *yawns again, and resumes his song.* PICKERING *returns,
with the contents of the letter-box in his hand.*

PICKERING Only circulars, and this coroneted billet-
  doux for you. (*He throws the circulars into the fender, and
  posts himself on the hearthrug, with his back to the grate.*)
HIGGINS (*glancing at the billet-doux*) Money-lender. (*He
  throws the letter after the circulars.*)

ELIZA *returns with a pair of large down-at-heel slippers. She
places them on the carpet before* HIGGINS, *and sits as before without a word.*

HIGGINS (*yawning again*) Oh Lord! What an evening!
  What a crew! What a silly tomfoolery! (*He raises his shoe
  to unlace it, and catches sight of the slippers. He stops unlacing
  and looks at them as if they had appeared there of their own
  accord.*) Oh! theyre there, are they? 20
PICKERING (*stretching himself*) Well, I feel a bit tired. It's
  been a long day. The garden party, a dinner party, and
  the reception! Rather too much of a good thing. But
  youve won your bet, Higgins. Eliza did the trick, and
  something to spare, eh?
HIGGINS (*fervently*) Thank God it's over!

ELIZA *flinches violently; but they take no notice of her; and she
recovers herself and sits stonily as before.*

PICKERING   Were you nervous at the garden par ? *I*
was. Eliza didnt seem a bit nervous.

HIGGINS   Oh, she wasnt nervous. I knew she'd be   'l
right. No: it's the strain of putting the job through al   30
these months that has told on me. It was interesting
enough at first, while we were at the phonetics; but
after that I got deadly sick of it. If I hadnt backed
myself to do it I should have chucked the whole thing
up two months ago. It was a silly notion: the whole
thing has been a bore.

PICKERING   Oh come! the garden party was frightfully
exciting. My heart began beating like anything.

HIGGINS   Yes, for the first three minutes. But when I saw
we were going to win hands down, I felt like a bear in   40
a cage, hanging about doing nothing. The dinner was
worse: sitting gorging there for over an hour, with nobody but a damned fool of a fashionable woman to talk
to! I tell you, Pickering, never again for me. No more
artificial duchesses. The whole thing has been simple
purgatory.

PICKERING   Youve never been broken in properly to the
social routine. (*Strolling over to the piano*) I rather enjoy
dipping into it occasionally myself: it makes me feel
young again. Anyhow, it was a great success: an im-   50
mense success. I was quite frightened once or twice because Eliza was doing it so well. You see, lots of the
real people cant do it at all: theyre such fools that they
think style comes by nature to people in their position;
and so they never learn. Theres always something pro-
fessional about doing a thing superlatively well.

HIGGINS   Yes: thats what drives me mad: the silly people
dont know their own silly business. (*Rising*) However,
it's over and done with; and now I can go to bed at last
without dreading tomorrow.   60

Eliza's beauty becomes murderous.

PICKERING I think I shall turn in too. Still, it's been a great occasion: a triumph for you. Goodnight. (*He goes.*)

HIGGINS (*following him*) Goodnight. (*Over his shoulder, at the door*) Put out the lights, Eliza; and tell Mrs Pearce not to make coffee for me in the morning: I'll take tea. (*He goes out.*)

ELIZA *tries to control herself and feel indifferent as she rises and walks across to the hearth to switch off the lights. By the time she gets there she is on the point of screaming. She sits down in Higgins's chair and holds on hard to the arms. Finally she gives way and flings herself furiously on the floor, raging.*

HIGGINS (*in despairing wrath outside*) What the devil have I done with my slippers? (*He appears at the door.*)

LIZA (*snatching up the slippers, and hurling them at him one after the other with all her force*) There are your slippers. And there. Take your slippers; and may you never have a day's luck with them! 70

HIGGINS (*astounded*) What on earth –! (*He comes to her.*) Whats the matter? Get up. (*He pulls her up.*) Anything wrong?

LIZA (*breathless*) Nothing wrong – with you. Ive won your bet for you, havnt I? Thats enough for you. *I* dont matter, I suppose.

HIGGINS You won my bet! You! Presumptuous insect! *I* won it. What did you throw those slippers at me for?

LIZA Because I wanted to smash your face. I'd like to kill you, you selfish brute. Why didnt you leave me 80 where you picked me out of – in the gutter? You thank God it's all over, and that now you can throw me back again there, do you? (*She crisps her fingers frantically.*)

HIGGINS (*looking at her in cool wonder*) The creature is nervous, after all.

LIZA (*gives a suffocated scream of fury, and instinctively darts her nails at his face*)!!

HIGGINS (*catching her wrists*) Ah! would you? Claws in, you cat. How dare you shew your temper to me? Sit down and be quiet. (*He throws her roughly into the easy-chair.*)

LIZA (*crushed by superior strength and weight*) Whats to become of me? Whats to become of me?   90

HIGGINS How the devil do I know whats to become of you? What does it matter what becomes of you?

LIZA You dont care. I know you dont care. You wouldnt care if I was dead. I'm nothing to you – not so much as them slippers.

HIGGINS (*thundering*) Those slippers.

LIZA (*with bitter submission*) Those slippers. I didnt think it made any difference now.

George Bernard Shaw (1912)

1 What differences are revealed here between the characters of Higgins and Pickering? Which of the men do you prefer?
2 Why is Eliza so unhappy and angry in this scene?
3 Explain in detail the importance of the *slippers* in this exchange. What use is Shaw making of this prop?

In the episode quoted above, Higgins's slippers come to assume a certain symbolic significance. A prop is being used to stand for or suggest a particular set of *attitudes*. In the final extract in this section, however – from *The School for Scandal* by Richard Brinsley Sheridan – a prop is being used as an essential part of the scene's *action*. It is as crucial to the comedy of the passage as the characters themselves.

Lady Teazle, flirtatious wife of the elderly Sir Peter Teazle, is in the library at the home of the hypocritical Joseph Surface whom she believes to be in love with her. In fact, he is pursuing Maria, Sir Peter's wealthy ward. Maria's other suitor is Joseph's attractive brother Charles, whom Sir Peter wrongly suspects of being involved with Lady Teazle. At the beginning of the scene, the audience's attention was drawn to a large screen in front of the window. Now read on.

The School for Scandal

JOSEPH SURFACE Then, by this hand, which he is unworthy of— (*Taking her hand*)

Enter SERVANT.

'Sdeath, you blockhead – what do you want?

SERVANT I beg your pardon, sir, but I thought you would not choose Sir Peter to come up without announcing him.

JOSEPH SURFACE Sir Peter! – Oons – the devil!

LADY TEAZLE Sir Peter! O Lud – I'm ruined – I'm ruined!

SERVANT Sir, 'twasn't I let him in. 10

LADY TEAZLE Oh! I'm quite undone! What will become of me? Now, Mr. Logic – Oh! he's on the stairs – I'll get behind here – and if ever I'm so imprudent again— (*Goes behind the screen*)

JOSEPH SURFACE Give me that book. (*Sits down.* SERVANT *pretends to adjust his hair.*)

Enter SIR PETER

SIR PETER TEAZLE Aye, ever improving himself – Mr. Surface, Mr. Surface—

JOSEPH SURFACE Oh! my dear Sir Peter, I beg your pardon – (*Gaping – throws away the book.*) – I have been dozing over a stupid book. – Well, I am much obliged to you for this call. You haven't been here, I believe, 20 since I fitted up this room. – Books, you know, are the only things in which I am a coxcomb.

SIR PETER TEAZLE 'Tis very neat indeed. – Well, well,

that's proper; and you can make even your screen a
source of knowledge – hung, I perceive, with maps?

JOSEPH SURFACE Oh, yes, I find great use in that screen.

SIR PETER TEAZLE I dare say you must, certainly, when
you want to find anything in a hurry.

JOSEPH SURFACE Aye, or to hide anything in a hurry
either. (Aside)   30

SIR PETER TEAZLE Well, I have a little private
business—

JOSEPH SURFACE You need not stay (to the SERVANT).

SERVANT No, sir.   Exit

JOSEPH SURFACE Here's a chair, Sir Peter – I beg—

SIR PETER TEAZLE Well, now we are alone, there is a
subject, my dear friend, on which I wish to unburthen
my mind to you – a point of the greatest moment to my
peace; in short, my dear friend, Lady Teazle's conduct
of late has made me extremely unhappy.   40

JOSEPH SURFACE Indeed! I am very sorry to hear it.

SIR PETER TEAZLE Aye, 'tis too plain she has not the
least regard for me; but, what's worse, I have pretty
good authority to suppose she has formed an attach-
ment to another.

JOSEPH SURFACE Indeed! you astonish me!

SIR PETER TEAZLE Yes; and, between ourselves, I think
I've discovered the person.

JOSEPH SURFACE How! you alarm me exceedingly.

SIR PETER TEAZLE Aye, my dear friend, I knew you   50
would sympathize with me!

JOSEPH SURFACE Yes – believe me, Sir Peter, such a dis-
covery would hurt just as much as it would you.

SIR PETER TEAZLE I am convinced of it. – Ah! it is a
happiness to have a friend whom we can trust even
with one's family secrets. But have you no guess who I
mean?

JOSEPH SURFACE I haven't the most distant idea. It can't
be Sir Benjamin Backbite!

SIR PETER TEAZLE Oh, no! What say you to Charles?   60

JOSEPH SURFACE My brother! impossible!

SIR PETER TEAZLE Oh! my dear friend, the goodness of your own heart misleads you. You judge of others by yourself.

JOSEPH SURFACE Certainly, Sir Peter, the heart that is conscious of its own integrity is ever slow to credit another's treachery.

SIR PETER TEAZLE True – but your brother has no sentiment – you never hear him talk so.

JOSEPH SURFACE Yet, I can't but think Lady Teazle herself has too much principle.   70

SIR PETER TEAZLE Aye, – but what is principle against the flattery of a handsome, lively young fellow?

JOSEPH SURFACE That's very true.

SIR PETER TEAZLE And there's, you know, the difference of our ages makes it very improbable that she should have any very great affection for me; and if she were to be frail, and I were to make it public, why the town would only laugh at me, the foolish old bachelor, who had married a girl.   80

JOSEPH SURFACE That's true, to be sure – they *would* laugh.

SIR PETER TEAZLE Laugh – aye, and make ballads, and paragraphs, and the devil knows what of me.

JOSEPH SURFACE No – you must never make it public.

SIR PETER TEAZLE But then again – that the nephew of my old friend, Sir Oliver, should be the person to attempt such a wrong, hurts me more nearly.

JOSEPH SURFACE Aye, there's the point. When ingratitude barbs the dart of injury, the wound has double   90 danger in it.

SIR PETER TEAZLE Aye – I, that was, in a manner, left his guardian; in whose house he had been so often entertained; who never in my life denied him – my advice.

JOSEPH SURFACE Oh, 'tis not to be credited. There may
be a man capable of such baseness, to be sure; but, for
my part, till you can give me positive proofs, I cannot
but doubt it. However, if it should be proved on him,
he is no longer a brother of mine – I disclaim kindred   100
with him: for the man who can break the laws of hospi-
tality, and tempt the wife of his friend, deserves to be
branded as the pest of society.

SIR PETER TEAZLE What a difference there is betweeen
you! What noble sentiments!

JOSEPH SURFACE Yet, I cannot suspect Lady Teazle's
honour.

SIR PETER TEAZLE I am sure I wish to think well of her,
and to remove all ground of quarrel between us. She
has lately reproached me more than once with having   110
made no settlement on her; and, in our last quarrel,
she almost hinted that she should not break her heart if
I was dead. Now, as we seem to differ in our ideas of
expense, I have resolved she shall have her own way,
and be her own mistress in that respect for the future;
and if I were to die, she will find I have not been in-
attentive to her interest while living. Here, my friend,
are the drafts of two deeds, which I wish to have your
opinion on. By one, she will enjoy eight hundred a year
independent while I live; and, by the other, the bulk of   120
my fortune at my death.

JOSEPH SURFACE This conduct, Sir Peter, is indeed truly
generous. – I wish it may not corrupt my pupil.
(Aside.)

SIR PETER TEAZLE Yes, I am determined she shall have
no cause to complain, though I would not have her
acquainted with the latter instance of my affection yet
awhile.

JOSEPH SURFACE Nor I, if I could help it. (Aside)

SIR PETER TEAZLE And now, my dear friend, if you

please, we will talk over the situation of your affairs   130
with Maria.

JOSEPH SURFACE (*softly*) – Oh, no, Sir Peter; another
time, if you please.

SIR PETER TEAZLE   I am sensibly chagrined at the little
progress you seem to make in her affections.

JOSEPH SURFACE   I beg you will not mention it. What are
my disappointments when your happiness is in debate!
(*Softly.*) – 'Sdeath, I shall be ruined every way. (*Aside*)

SIR PETER TEAZLE   And though you are so averse to my
acquainting Lady Teazle with your passion for Maria,   140
I'm sure she's not your enemy in the affair.

JOSEPH SURFACE   Pray, Sir Peter, now, oblige me. I am
really too much affected by the subject we have been
speaking of, to bestow a thought on my own concerns.
The man who is entrusted with his friend's distresses
can never—

Enter SERVANT

Well, sir?

SERVANT   Your brother, sir, is speaking to a gentleman
in the street, and says he knows you are within.

JOSEPH SURFACE   'Sdeath, blockhead, I'm not within –   150
I'm out for the day.

SIR PETER TEAZLE   Stay – hold – a thought has struck
me: – you shall be at home.

JOSEPH SURFACE   Well, well, let him up. (*Exit* SERVANT)
He'll interrupt Sir Peter, however. (*Aside*)

SIR PETER TEAZLE   Now, my good friend, oblige me, I
entreat you. Before Charles comes, let me conceal myself somewhere – then do you tax him on the point we
have been talking, and his answer may satisfy me at
once.   160

JOSEPH SURFACE   Oh, fie, Sir Peter! would you have me
join in so mean a trick? – to trepan my brother too?

SIR PETER TEAZLE   Nay, you tell me you are sure he is innocent; if so, you do him the greatest service by giving him an opportunity to clear himself, and you will set my heart at rest. Come, you shall not refuse me: here, behind this screen will be – Hey! what the devil! there seems to be one listener there already – I'll swear I saw a petticoat!

JOSEPH SURFACE   Ha! ha! ha! Well, this is ridiculous   170
enough. I'll tell you, Sir Peter, though I hold a man of intrigue to be a most despicable character, yet, you know, it does not follow that one is to be an absolute Joseph either! Hark'ee, 'tis a little French milliner – a silly rogue that plagues me, – and having some character to lose, on your coming, sir, she ran behind the screen.

SIR PETER TEAZLE   Ah! you rogue! But, egad, she has overheard all I have been saying of my wife.

JOSEPH SURFACE   Oh, 'twill never go any farther, you   180
may depend upon it.

SIR PETER TEAZLE   No! then, faith, let her hear it out. – Here's a closet will do as well.

JOSEPH SURFACE   Well, go in there.

SIR PETER TEAZLE   Sly rogue! sly rogue! (*Going into the closet*)

JOSEPH SURFACE   A narrow escape, indeed! and a curious situation I'm in, to part man and wife in this manner.

LADY TEAZLE   (*peeping*) – Couldn't I steal off?

JOSEPH SURFACE   Keep close, my angel!

SIR PETER TEAZLE   (*peeping*) Joseph, tax him home.   190

JOSEPH SURFACE   Back, my dear friend!

LADY TEAZLE   Couldn't you lock Sir Peter in?

JOSEPH SURFACE   Be still, my life!

SIR PETER TEAZLE   (*peeping*) You're sure the little milliner won't blab?

JOSEPH SURFACE   In, in, my good Sir Peter. – 'Fore Gad, I wish I had a key to the door.

Enter CHARLES SURFACE.

CHARLES SURFACE   Holla! brother, what has been the matter? Your fellow would not let me up at first. What! have you had a Jew or a wench with you?   200

JOSEPH SURFACE   Neither, brother, I assure you.

CHARLES SURFACE   But what has made Sir Peter steal off? I thought he had been with you.

JOSEPH SURFACE   He *was*, brother; but hearing you were coming, he did not choose to stay.

Richard Brinsley Sheridan (1777)

1   Explain how Joseph manages to delude Sir Peter into believing him honest and uncorrupt in this scene.

2   Why does Joseph speak 'softly' at line 132, and attempt to change the topic of conversation?

3   Show how Sheridan uses the screen and the closet to highlight the farce of this episode.

4   What is the irony of Joseph's remark at line 26 ('I find great use in that screen')? What similar examples of irony can you find?

5   How do you imagine this scene will end?

Assignment

Make a special study of the use of set and props in *Oh What a Lovely War* (1963), co-written by Theatre Workshop, and of the use of lighting and sound in *Black Comedy* (1965) by Peter Shaffer.

5 Playing at life
How plays make us think

By reading or watching plays we can learn a great deal about human relationships, about the kinds of conflicts and dilemmas that people may encounter in their lives, and about the motives that cause them to behave in the ways that they do. These insights are a very valuable experience, and part of the special pleasure that plays can offer us. For they do not just increase our understanding of *other* people. They also encourage us to explore and assess our *own* feelings and priorities.

As an example of the power of plays to provoke a deeply personal reaction from readers or an audience, read the following extract and then think very carefully about the dilemma facing the central character, Isabella. The extract comes from Shakespeare's *Measure for Measure*. The play is set in Vienna, where morality has become very lax. In the absence of the Duke who governs the city, Angelo (his Deputy) has enforced stringent laws to 'clean up' Vienna. Claudio has been sentenced to death for making his fiancée (Juliet) pregnant. Claudio's sister, Isabella, who is a novice nun, has gone to plead with Angelo for his life. She is now visiting Claudio in prison to tell him the outcome of the interview.

Measure for Measure

CLAUDIO
Now, sister, what's the comfort?

ISABELLA
Why,
As all comforts are; most good, most good, indeed.

Lord Angelo, having affairs to heaven,
Intends you for his swift ambassador,
Where you shall be an everlasting leiger.
Therefore, your best appointment make with speed;
To-morrow you set on.

CLAUDIO

Is there no remedy?

ISABELLA

None, but such remedy as, to save a head,
To cleave a heart in twain.

CLAUDIO

But is there any? 10

ISABELLA

Yes, brother, you may live:
There is a devilish mercy in the judge,
If you'll implore it, that will free your life,
But fetter you till death.

CLAUDIO

Perpetual durance?

ISABELLA

Ay, just; perpetual durance, a restraint,
Though all the world's vastidity you had,
To a determin'd scope.

CLAUDIO

But in what nature?

ISABELLA

In such a one as, you consenting to't,
Would bark your honour from that trunk you bear,
And leave you naked.

CLAUDIO

Let me know the point. 20

ISABELLA

O, I do fear thee, Claudio; and I quake,
Lest thou a feverous life shouldst entertain,
And six or seven winters more respect
Than a perpetual honour. Dar'st thou die?
The sense of death is most in apprehension;
And the poor beetle that we tread upon
In corporal sufferance finds a pang as great
As when a giant dies.

CLAUDIO

Why give you me this shame?
Think you I can a resolution fetch
From flow'ry tenderness? If I must die,   30
I will encounter darkness as a bride
And hug it in mine arms.

ISABELLA

There spake my brother; there my father's grave
Did utter forth a voice. Yes, thou must die:
Thou art too noble to conserve a life
In base appliances. This outward-sainted deputy,
Whose settled visage and deliberate word
Nips youth i' th' head, and follies doth enew
As falcon doth the fowl, is yet a devil;
His filth within being cast, he would appear   40
A pond as deep as hell.

CLAUDIO

The precise Angelo!

ISABELLA

O, 'tis the cunning livery of hell
The damned'st body to invest and cover
In precise guards! Dost thou think, Claudio,
If I would yield him my virginity
Thou mightst be freed?

CLAUDIO

O heavens! it cannot be.

ISABELLA

Yes, he would give't thee, from this rank offence,
So to offend him still. This night's the time
That I should do what I abhor to name,
Or else thou diest to-morrow.

CLAUDIO

Thou shalt not do't.   50

ISABELLA

O, were it but my life!
I'd throw it down for your deliverance
As frankly as a pin.

CLAUDIO

Thanks, dear Isabel.

ISABELLA

Be ready, Claudio, for your death to-morrow.

CLAUDIO

Yes. Has he affections in him
That thus can make him bite the law by th' nose
When he would force it? Sure it is no sin;
Or of the deadly seven it is the least.

ISABELLA

Which is the least?

CLAUDIO

If it were damnable, he being so wise,   60
Why would he for the momentary trick
Be perdurably fin'd – O Isabel!

ISABELLA

What says my brother?

CLAUDIO

Death is a fearful thing.

ISABELLA

And shamed life a hateful.

CLAUDIO

Ay, but to die, and go we know not where;
To lie in cold obstruction, and to rot;
This sensible warm motion to become
A kneaded clod; and the delighted spirit
To bathe in fiery floods or to reside
In thrilling region of thick-ribbed ice;   70
To be imprison'd in the viewless winds,
And blown with restless violence round about
The pendent world; or to be worse than worst
Of those that lawless and incertain thought
Imagine howling – 'tis too horrible.
The weariest and most loathed worldly life
That age, ache, penury, and imprisonment,
Can lay on nature is a paradise
To what we fear of death.

ISABELLA

Alas, alas!

CLAUDIO

Sweet sister, let me live.   80
What sin you do to save a brother's life,
Nature dispenses with the deed so far
That it becomes a virtue.

ISABELLA

O you beast!
O faithless coward! O dishonest wretch!
Wilt thou be made a man out of my vice?
Is't not a kind of incest to take life
From thine own sister's shame? What should I think?

Heaven shield my mother play'd my father fair!
For such a warped slip of wilderness
Ne'er issu'd from his blood. Take my defiance;   90
Die; perish. Might but my bending down
Reprieve thee from thy fate, it should proceed.
I'll pray a thousand prayers for thy death,
No word to save thee.

CLAUDIO

Nay, hear me, Isabel.

ISABELLA

                O fie, fie, fie!
Thy sin's not accidental, but a trade.
Mercy to thee would prove itself a bawd;
'Tis best that thou diest quickly.

                    William Shakespeare (1603)

1   On what condition has Angelo agreed to free Claudio?
2   Explain why Isabella will not agree to this condition. Do you agree with her decision?
3   With whom do you sympathise most in this extract: Claudio or Isabella? Why?
4   What makes this such a powerful scene?

Ultimately, almost all plays evoke for us a particular vision of life and of the world in which we live. The vision may be a comic one. In other words, it may suggest that, although human beings themselves are often muddled or ridiculous, there is still a basic spirit of positive goodness in humanity that allows most of us to overcome evil and co-exist happily with others. Alternatively, the vision may be darker and more tragic. It may suggest that human beings are essentially lonely creatures, that ties between individuals are very superficial, and that there is no controlling force at work in the universe that we can trust to protect the good or punish the bad. More bleakly still, it may suggest that there *is* a force beyond man, but that that force is a hostile and threatening one, in the face of which human beings are reduced to mere puppets.

Waiting for Godot by Samuel Beckett is one of the most influential plays of the twentieth century, and is preoccupied almost totally with defining man's position within an incomprehensible and often alien universe. The play challenges us to question what we are doing with our lives, and what we hope to achieve from our existence. It focuses on two clown-like characters, Vladimir and Estragon, who return day after day to the same spot (a bare tree in a sterile landscape) waiting for someone they have never met and know only as 'Godot'. When Godot comes, they believe they will be 'saved'. But Godot never comes.

This extract is taken from the end of the play.

Waiting for Godot

VLADIMIR   Was I sleeping, while the others suffered? Am I sleeping now? Tomorrow, when I wake, or think I do, what shall I say of today? That with Estragon my friend, at this place, until the fall of night, I waited for Godot? That Pozzo passed, with his carrier, and that he spoke to us? Probably. But in all that what truth will there be? (ESTRAGON, *having struggled with his boots in vain, is dozing off again.* VLADIMIR *stares at him.*) He'll know nothing. He'll tell me about the blows he received and I'll give him a carrot. (*Pause.*) Astride of a   10 grave and a difficult birth. Down in the hole, lingeringly, the grave-digger puts on the forceps. We have time to grow old. The air is full of our cries. (*He listens.*) But habit is a great deadener. (*He looks again at* ESTRAGON.) At me too someone is looking, of me too someone is saying, he is sleeping, he knows nothing, let him sleep on. (*Pause.*) I can't go on! (*Pause.*) What have I said?

He goes feverishly to and fro, halts finally at extreme left, broods.
Enter BOY *right. He halts. Silence.*

BOY Mister . . . (VLADIMIR *turns.*) Mr. Albert . . .

VLADIMIR Off we go again. (*Pause.*) Do you not recognize me?   20

BOY No, sir.

VLADIMIR It wasn't you came yesterday.

BOY No, sir.

VLADIMIR This is your first time.

BOY Yes, sir.

Silence.

VLADIMIR You have a message from Mr. Godot.

BOY Yes, sir.

VLADIMIR He won't come this evening.

BOY No, sir.

VLADIMIR But he'll come tomorrow.   30

BOY Yes, sir.

VLADIMIR Without fail.

BOY Yes, sir.

Silence.

VLADIMIR Did you meet anyone?

BOY No, sir.

VLADIMIR Two other . . . (*he hesitates*) . . . men?

BOY I didn't see anyone, sir.

Silence.

VLADIMIR What does he do, Mr. Godot? (*Silence.*) Do you hear me?

BOY Yes, sir.   40

VLADIMIR Well?

BOY He does nothing sir.

Silence.

VLADIMIR How is your brother?

BOY   He's sick, sir.

VLADIMIR   Perhaps it was he came yesterday.

BOY   I don't know, sir.

Silence.

VLADIMIR (*softly*)   Has he a beard, Mr. Godot?

BOY   Yes, sir.

VLADIMIR   Fair or . . . (*he hesitates*) . . . or black?

BOY   I think it's white, sir.   50

Silence.

VLADIMIR   Christ have mercy on us!

Silence.

BOY   What am I to tell Mr. Godot, sir?

VLADIMIR   Tell him . . . (*he hesitates*) . . . tell him you saw
me and that . . . (*he hesitates*) . . . that you saw me.
(*Pause.* VLADIMIR *advances, the* BOY *recoils.* VLADIMIR *halts,
the* BOY *halts. With sudden violence.*) You're sure you saw
me, you won't come and tell me tomorrow that you
never saw me!

Silence. VLADIMIR *makes a sudden spring forward, the* BOY
*avoids him and exit running. Silence. The sun sets, the moon rises.
As in Act I.* VLADIMIR *stands motionless and bowed.* ESTRAGON
*wakes, takes off his boots, gets up with one in each hand and goes
and puts them down centre front, then goes towards* VLADIMIR.

ESTRAGON   What's wrong with you?

VLADIMIR   Nothing.

ESTRAGON   I'm going.

VLADIMIR   So am I.   60

ESTRAGON   Was I long asleep?

VLADIMIR   I don't know.

Silence

ESTRAGON   Where shall we go?

VLADIMIR	Not far.
ESTRAGON	Oh yes, let's go far away from here.
VLADIMIR	We can't.
ESTRAGON	Why not?
VLADIMIR	We have to come back tomorrow.
ESTRAGON	What for?

VLADIMIR   To wait for Godot.

ESTRAGON   Ah! (*Silence.*) He didn't come?

VLADIMIR   No.

ESTRAGON   And now it's too late.

VLADIMIR   Yes, now it's night.

ESTRAGON   And if we dropped him? (*Pause.*) If we dropped him?

VLADIMIR   He'd punish us. (*Silence. He looks at the tree.*) Everything's dead but the tree.

ESTRAGON (*looking at the tree*)   What is it?

VLADIMIR   It's the tree.

ESTRAGON   Yes, but what kind?

VLADIMIR   I don't know. A willow.

ESTRAGON *draws* VLADIMIR *towards the tree. They stand motionless before it. Silence.*

ESTRAGON   Why don't we hang ourselves?

VLADIMIR   With what?

ESTRAGON   You haven't got a bit of rope?

VLADIMIR   No.

ESTRAGON   Then we can't.

Silence.

VLADIMIR   Let's go.

ESTRAGON   Wait, there's my belt.

VLADIMIR   It's too short.

ESTRAGON   You could hang on to my legs.

VLADIMIR   And who'd hang on to mine?

ESTRAGON   True.

VLADIMIR   Show me all the same. (ESTRAGON *loosens the cord*

*that holds up his trousers which, much too big for him, fall
about his ankles. They look at the cord.*) It might do at a
pinch. But is it strong enough?

ESTRAGON   We'll soon see. Here.

*They each take an end of the cord and pull. It breaks. They almost
fall.*

VLADIMIR   Not worth a curse.

Silence.

ESTRAGON   You say we have to come back tomorrow?   100
VLADIMIR   Yes.
ESTRAGON   Then we can bring a good bit of rope.
VLADIMIR   Yes.

Silence.

ESTRAGON   Didi.
VLADIMIR   Yes.
ESTRAGON   I can't go on like this.
VLADIMIR   That's what you think.
ESTRAGON   If we parted? That might be better for us.
VLADIMIR   We'll hang ourselves tomorrow. (*Pause.*) Un-
less Godot comes.   110
ESTRAGON   And if he comes?
VLADIMIR   We'll be saved.

VLADIMIR *takes off his hat* (*Lucky's*), *peers inside it, feels about
inside it, shakes it, knocks on the crown, puts it on again.*

ESTRAGON   Well? Shall we go?
VLADIMIR   Pull on your trousers.
ESTRAGON   What?
VLADIMIR   Pull on your trousers.
ESTRAGON   You want me to pull off my trousers?
VLADIMIR   Pull ON your trousers.
ESTRAGON (*realizing his trousers are down*)   True. (*He pulls up
his trousers.*)

VLADIMIR Well? Shall we go? 120
ESTRAGON Yes, let's go.

They do not move.

CURTAIN

Samuel Beckett (Faber & Faber, 1955)

1 Discuss the ideas in Vladimir's first speech. What view of existence does this speech give?
2 What do you learn about Godot in this extract? What do you think he represents?
3 Why does Godot not come? Do you think Vladimir and Estragon are foolish or brave to continue to wait?
4 Do you consider Vladimir's and Estragon's inability to hang themselves to be tragic or comic?
5 The play ends with the characters saying that they want to move and yet seemingly unable to do so. What does this suggest to you about man's position in this world?
6 Do you think that Beckett is painting too gloomy a picture of life here? If so, why?

In considering man's place in the scheme of things, many playwrights have been drawn to the metaphor of an actor on a stage – someone who plays the part that has been scripted for him, but whose role is inevitably brief and ultimately insignificant. Look at the following speeches from two separate plays by Shakespeare.

As You Like It

JAQUES
               All the world's stage,
  And all the men and women, merely players;
  They have their exits and their entrances,

And one man in his time plays many parts,
His acts being seven ages. At first the infant,
Mewling, and puking in the nurse's arms.
Then, the whining school-boy, with his satchel
And shining morning face, creeping like snail
Unwillingly to school. And then the lover,
Sighing like furnace, with a woeful ballad   10
Made to his mistress' eyebrow. Then, a soldier,
Full of strange oaths, and bearded like the pard,
Jealous in honour, sudden, and quick in quarrel,
Seeking the bubble reputation
Even in the cannon's mouth. And then, the justice,
In fair round belly with good capon lined,
With eyes severe, and beard of formal cut,
Full of wise saws, and modern instances;
And so he plays his part. The sixth age shifts
Into the lean and slippered pantaloon,   20
With spectacles on nose, and pouch on side,
His youthful hose, well saved, a world too wide
For his shrunk shank; and his big manly voice,
Turning again toward childish treble, pipes
And whistles in his sound. Last scene of all,
That ends this strange eventful history,
Is second childishness, and mere oblivion,
Sans teeth, sans eyes, sans taste, sans everything.

William Shakespeare (1600)

Macbeth

MACBETH

Tomorrow, and tomorrow, and tomorrow,
Creeps in this petty pace from day to day,
To the last syllable of recorded time;
And all our yesterdays have lighted fools

The way to dusty death. Out, out, brief candle!
Life's but a walking shadow, a poor player
That struts and frets his hour upon the stage
And then is heard no more. It is a tale
Told by an idiot, full of sound and fury,
Signifying nothing.   10

William Shakespeare (1606)

1 What central ideas do these speeches have in common?
2 What are the 'seven ages' described by Jaques in the first
   of these extracts? Which seems to you the least attractive?
3 What does Macbeth suggest by 'struts and frets' in the
   second extract, line 7?
4 In what ways do these two speeches differ?
6 Which (if either) do you find more persuasive? Why?

In 1967, the modern dramatist Tom Stoppard based a whole
play around the life/acting metaphor. The play is *Rosencrantz
and Guildenstern Are Dead*, and it takes as its two main figures
two very insignificant minor characters from Shakespeare's
Hamlet. Rosencrantz and Guildenstern have had no part in
writing the script of *Hamlet*. Indeed, they have never even *seen*
the whole script. Their duty is simply to perform on cue, which
includes going to their deaths as directed. They have no free
will. Immensely frustrated yet struggling to do their best and
to make sense of roles that they cannot possibly understand,
they are both comic and dignified. Perhaps, Stoppard suggests,
our own position is not so very different.

This extract comes from the end of the play, and seems a
fitting point at which to end this section. The two characters
have suddenly realised that they are doomed. The boat that
they thought would take them to safety has actually taken
them to their deaths. Read the passage carefully. What is your
response to it?

Rosencrantz and Guildenstern Are Dead

GUILDENSTERN (*quietly*) Where we went wrong was getting on a boat. We can move, of course, change direction, rattle about, but our movement is contained within a larger one that carries us along as inexorably as the wind and current. . . .

ROSENCRANTZ They had it in for us, didn't they? Right from the beginning. Who'd have thought that we were so important?

GUILDENSTERN But why? Was it all for this? Who are we that so much should converge on our little deaths? (*In anguish to the* PLAYER.) Who are *we*?   10

PLAYER You are Rosencrantz and Guildenstern. That's enough.

GUILDENSTERN No – it is not enough. To be told so little – to such an end – and still, finally, to be denied an explanation. . . .

PLAYER In our experience, most things end in death.

GUILDENSTERN (*fear, vengeance, scorn*) Your experience? – *Actors!*

(*He snatches a dagger from the* PLAYER's *belt and holds the point at the* PLAYER's *throat: the* PLAYER *backs and* GUILDENSTERN *advances, speaking more quietly.*)

I'm talking about death – and you've never   20
experienced *that*. And you cannot *act* it. You die a thousand casual deaths – with none of that intensity which squeezes out life . . . and no blood runs cold anywhere. Because even as you die you know that you will come back in a different hat. But no one gets up after *death* – there is no applause – there is only silence and some second-hand clothes, and that's – *death* –

Tom Stoppard (Faber & Faber, 1967)

Assignment

Read *Doctor Faustus* (c.1590) by Christopher Marlowe. To what extent do you sympathise with Faustus in this play? To what extent do you consider him responsible for his fate?

Chronological table of extracts

Acknowledgements

We are grateful to the following for permission to reproduce copyright material:

Associated Book Publishers (UK) Ltd for an extract from pp 61–66 *The Birthday Party* by Harold Pinter (pub Methuen London, 1958); Faber and Faber Ltd for extracts from *Waiting for Godot* by Samuel Beckett (1955), *The Philanthropist* by Christopher Hampton (1970), *Look Back in Anger* by John Osborne (1956), *A Resounding Tinkle* by N F Simpson (1957) and *Jumpers* by Tom Stoppard (1972); Heinemann Educational Books Ltd for an extract from *A Man for All Seasons* by Robert Bolt (1964); the author's agents for an extract from *The Browning Version* by Terence Rattigan (pub Hamish Hamilton/Samuel French Ltd 1948).

Longman Study Texts General editor: Richard Adams

Novels and stories

Jane Austen
Emma
Pride and Prejudice
Charlotte Brontë
Jane Eyre
Emily Brontë
Wuthering Heights
Charles Dickens
Great Expectations
Hard Times
Oliver Twist
George Eliot
Silas Marner
The Mill on the Floss
Nadine Gordimer
July's People
Thomas Hardy
Far From the Madding Crowd
The Mayor of Casterbridge
Aldous Huxley
Brave New World
Robin Jenkins
The Cone-Gatherers
D H Lawrence
Sons and Lovers
Somerset Maugham
Short Stories
George Orwell
Animal Farm
Nineteen Eighty-Four
Alan Paton
Cry, The Beloved Country
Paul Scott
Staying On
Mark Twain
Huckleberry Finn
H G Wells
The History of Mr Polly
Virginia Woolf
To the Lighthouse

Plays

Oliver Goldsmith
She Stoops to Conquer
Ben Jonson
Volpone
Christopher Marlowe
Doctor Faustus
J B Priestley
An Inspector Calls
Terence Rattigan
The Winslow Boy
Willy Russell
Educating Rita
Peter Shaffer
Amadeus
Equus
The Royal Hunt of the Sun
William Shakespeare
Macbeth
The Merchant of Venice
Romeo and Juliet
Bernard Shaw
Androcles and the Lion
Arms and the Man
Caesar and Cleopatra
The Devil's Disciple
Major Barbara
Pygmalion
Saint Joan
Richard Brinsley Sheridan
The Rivals
The School for Scandal
John Webster
The Duchess of Malfi
The White Devil
Oscar Wilde
The Importance of Being Earnest

Editor: George MacBeth
Poetry for Today
Editor: Michael Marland
Short Stories for Today